Presented to

T8 marl flm . 7 . r
_____

By

_____

On the Occasion of

Mother's Dot
_____

Date

May 8' 2010
_____

THE QUILT OF LIFE

A Patchwork of Devotional Thoughts

THE QUILT OF LIFE

A Patchwork of Devotional Thoughts

Mary Tatem

BARBOUR
PUBLISHING

DEDICATION

To my mother,
Louisa Griner McCormick,
who taught me at an early age that God
establishes patterns for His people's lives.
She's an inspiring example of maintaining a thankful heart
as we follow His design for us.

ACKNOWLEDGMENTS

I want to thank the many gracious people who shared their stories about quilts with me. I'd especially like to thank Nancy Gloss, the owner of Nancy's Calico Patch, and Mary Frances Ballard, both of whom patiently answered my questions and supplied resources for my research. A large thank-you goes to my son, Andrew Tatem, who gave his time and skill to critique the book.

WELCOME TO THE
WARMTH OF QUILTS

Quilts wrap our hearts in warm emotions. They represent time, energy, and planning. The hours required to create a quilt offer plenty of opportunity to think about the person for whom it is intended. When combining needlework with prayer, a quilter catches a glimpse of the love of God, who stitches the fabric of our lives with His plans and purposes for our good and not our destruction.

A quilt bridges the generation gap by connecting people from the past with people yet to come. Perhaps that longing to participate in the future gives quilting its strong appeal. A quilt represents a reach for immortality. We stitch hoping our lives, our personalities, our struggles, and our joys will find a place of remembrance in the minds and emotions of others.

While reading these pages, tap into the heartbeat of our Creator, the Master quilter, who designs our lives using His perfect pattern. Skillfully placing the lights and darks of our lives, He joins the mountains and valleys of our days to make us into comforters who warm others.

Relax with this book for a few moments each week allowing the thread of God's truths to beautify and stabilize your life while you become God's work of art.

Note: If you're a quilter yourself (or aspire to be one), don't miss the helpful "Quilting Tips" section beginning on page 241!

SURPRISE CHANGES

O ne only needed to step inside the scarred front door of the middle school to feel the poverty and neglect of the youngsters who attended it. In this school learning and sharing were not priorities. The children's days were dedicated to defending their rights. In the middle of this discouraging environment, Mary Fran tried day after day to teach home economics. No one cared. One day she arrived in class carrying a huge shopping bag full of colorful fabric scraps. When she dumped them on the table, curious eighth graders crowded around.

"Has anyone ever heard of safe houses for battered women?" she asked. They had. Some even spoke of relatives who had spent time in one of these havens for women who, beaten by husbands or boyfriends, feared for their lives.

"I'm looking for volunteers to make quilts to put on the beds at a battered women's safe house. I'm hoping these quilts will warm and comfort some women who are afraid and in despair."

To Mary Fran's delight, four girls and one boy volunteered. They enjoyed selecting bright and cheerful prints from the piles of donated materials. Their teacher marveled at the conscientious efforts her students made to cut even squares. The room buzzed with excitement the day they laid the squares out on tables to decide what arrangement of the various colors and patterns looked best. After a few suggestions, the students were careful not to put all the red tones at one end and all the yellows at the other. For the first time in their lives, they were striving for artistry. Next, they used serger machines at the school to stitch the squares together into five quilts. As the squares of the top were sewn to the backing and batting material, they chattered with pride over their attractive quilts. The children enjoyed a rare sense of accomplishment.

The following morning, Mary Fran arrived in her classroom to discover someone had stolen one quilt overnight. She dreaded telling the class. The group of kids who had so far only exhibited a "what's in it for me" attitude amazed her with their response. The children agreed with a girl who said, "Well, if someone took it, maybe they really needed a quilt to keep them warm and show them some people care about what happens to other people."

When we use God's pattern for living, God often gives us surprising little twists of benefits beyond what we expected. By giving to others, these thirteen-year-old children shook off their "me first or I get even" attitude to develop an important character trait—generosity. They learned to consider the needs of others ahead of their own desires. When we give to God, He returns to us growth and maturity.

∽

GOD'S PATTERN

When we practice giving to others,
God changes us, and we gain the unexpected blessing of
receiving extra joy as we become more like Christ.

THE UNEXPECTED

For I know the thoughts that I think toward you,
saith the LORD, thoughts of peace,
and not of evil, to give you an expected end.
JEREMIAH 29:11 KJV

Anne breathed in the sweet smell of powder mixed with clean baby. She gave the soft, round bottom a quick pat before she fastened her new daughter's diaper. She snuggled the baby close, reveling in motherhood. Her joy dimmed only a moment at the thought that had haunted her the entire nine months of her pregnancy. How could a mother give up her little child? Anne's mother had done just that: She had left her husband and then three-year-old Anne to find a life of "fun," so the story went.

"I'll never abandon you, little one," Anne murmured as she laid the sleeping baby in her crib. "I'll always make sure you know I'm glad you were born."

A short time later, the doorbell rang, and the postman handed Anne a bulky package. Her heart leaped at the return address. She had never received anything from her mother's address. Her throat squeezed and tears threatened. If she had cried for her mama long ago, she didn't remember it anymore. All she ever felt was an empty place, one of not quite belonging in spite of all the love her aunt and uncle had given her.

Slowly she snipped the tape and pulled the paper away to reveal a worn, somewhat faded baby quilt. Pinned to it was a note that read: "This was made for you when you were born, by my mother, your grandmother. I wanted you to have it for your new baby. Mother."

Anne spread the quilt over the nearby table. She fingered the carefully embroidered animals in each corner of the lovely blending of pink fabrics. Tears mingled with laughter as she looked at her grandmother's handiwork. Someone had rejoiced she was born after all. Her grandmother cared enough to spend hours cutting, piecing, and sewing little pieces of fabric into a pretty design to celebrate her birth. She could picture a gray-headed lady sitting in a rocker stitching love into the fabric. Anne hugged the quilt to herself and danced around the room singing her own made-up little tune. "Someone was glad I was born. Someone was glad."

Smiling, she tiptoed into the baby's room and gently laid the quilt over the sleeping form. Her daughter stretched a minute and then settled back to sleep. "I'm glad you are here, little one. When I wrap you in this quilt, I'll remember someone cared about me."

No one is unwanted by God. Even before our birth, He cared about us. His love for His people is constant and never fails. He has wrapped us in His love even when we don't feel it. "But the plans of the LORD stand firm forever, the purposes of his heart through all generations" (Psalm 33:11 NIV).

GOD'S PATTERN
Even if a person feels unwanted,
God has a special plan for every life.

GALLOPING HORSES

You, then, why do you judge your brother?
Or why do you look down on your brother?
For we will all stand before God's judgment seat.
ROMANS 14:10 NIV

I would never have stuck to quilting if it weren't for my Grandma Brown." Laura stood by her quilt hung at the quilt festival. "My other grandmother, Grandma Winters, always won first prize in quilt competitions. If she didn't think it was good enough to win, she didn't enter it. She demanded perfection from herself, ripping out and reworking so she could win. As a child I didn't notice the subtle differences that made one quilt win over another.

"'Grandma, let me stitch a little on your quilt,' I'd ask, but I was always given a different square for practice. Then Grandma checked it and turned it over to examine the stitches on the back, clucking her tongue all the while. She'd hand it back to me, telling me to rip it out and do it again. I spent more time ripping than sewing at her house. I hated it.

"But at Grandma Brown's house, she'd look at my work and call out to my mother or Grandpa, 'Will you look at Laura's quilting! She improves every day. Why, I declare, she is becoming a little seamstress.'

"When I'd get discouraged because the points and edges of my pieces weren't matching up exactly right, she'd dismiss the problem with a wave of her hand saying, 'You'll never notice it on the back of a galloping horse.'"

Isn't that a wonderful way for us to look at the flaws in each other? Why point out the problems a person has? They are probably painfully aware of them anyway. If we dwell on another's faults, we forget to notice his or her good qualities, and we may become discouraged from offering them friendship and acceptance. As we gallop through our days, life goes too fast to waste time criticizing. Let's concentrate on noticing the improvements and strengths in everyone. Encouraging words create growth and determination to improve.

GOD'S PATTERN

God is a perfect judge.
He understands all the facets of
our behavior and responses.
His bountiful mercy balances His judgment.

WONDERING WHY
THEY WANDER

These commandments that I give you today
are to be upon your hearts.
Impress them on your children.
Talk about them when you sit at home
and when you walk along the road,
when you lie down and when you get up.
DEUTERONOMY 6:6–7 NIV

Years ago in the United States, a quilt pattern called Wandering Foot enjoyed popularity because its attractive design was relatively easy to piece. Later a folktale linked the pattern with rebellious children leaving home much earlier than expected. Searching for explanations for why their children left, disappointed parents began to blame the comforter dubbed Wandering Foot for their heartache. Eventually the superstition developed that if a child slept under a Wandering Foot quilt, the boy or girl would leave home at a young age. Understandably this pattern lost its appeal and was studiously avoided until some clever person renamed the pattern Turkey Tracks. The new name was associated with a common sight in rural America, removing the fears surrounding the motif, and the design enjoyed a renewal of favor. Kids could once again safely snuggle under its warm cover.

Christian parents rely on God's protective cover over their youngsters rather than troubling themselves with superstitions. They gear their daily conversations to include instructions about God. Any actions or events of the day are appropriate moments to reinforce the knowledge of God and His plans. By steady example and training, parents surround their children with God's designs for successful living. Even when a child is rebellious and makes poor choices, a parent who has taught his or her children about God's love finds peace. We know ultimately God will fulfill the promise of scripture: "Train a child in the way he should go, and when he is old he will not turn from it" (Proverbs 22:6 NIV).

GOD'S PATTERN
The family is God's plan for teaching
each new generation about His ways.
When we trust God to help us raise our children,
we are not tormented by superstitions.

OWNERSHIP

"Fear not, for I have redeemed you;
I have summoned you by name; you are mine."
ISAIAH 43:1 NIV

"Where's your name? Didn't you sign this wonderful quilt?" Beth asked Marie as she helped examine the quilt for any remnants of basting threads.

"I didn't think I would."

"Why not? Aren't you proud of it? You should be. It's a beautiful quilt, and you sure invested enough time in it. How long did it take to finish all this handwork?"

"Three years. I *am* proud of it; I know it's not perfect, but it's pretty."

Beth showed Marie a book full of lovely drawings for quilt labels. Marie traced one on a piece of muslin and colored the design with permanent-ink colored pens. Next she wrote her name, the date and place she completed the quilt, the reason she made it, and the name of the person she was giving it to.

"Your label will matter to someone a couple of generations from now," Beth said with satisfaction while Marie slip-stitched it to the back of the quilt at one corner. "This quilt says something about you. It's a piece of your history. I hope you're proud of your careful workmanship. Anyone would feel proud to own this quilt."

We are the careful workmanship of God, who created us. And He is pleased with His creation. We are not perfect, but He loves us anyway because He made us. He wants to polish what He made and make us more beautiful each day. When we allow Him to arrange the pieces of our lives, His plan, His pattern for us is more perfect than anything we can create on our own. The Bible tell us that He knows us so well He even knows how many hairs we have; yet He gladly proclaims His ownership of us and calls us by our name.

Isaiah 49:16 (NIV) says: "See, I have engraved you on the palms of my hands; your walls are ever before me." He writes His name on us when we accept Christ, and we are called by His name when we are called Christians, which means "little Christ."

GOD'S PATTERN

God loves us even when we know
we have not pleased Him.
He does not tire of working with us
and nudging us toward completion.

ALARM BUZZERS

*"But if you do warn the righteous man
not to sin and he does not sin,
he will surely live because he took warning,
and you will have saved yourself."*
EZEKIEL 3:21 NIV

Diane's heels clicked across the floor. Her pace mirrored her excitement. "Unbelievable!" she exclaimed as she entered the huge room in the museum where dozens of Baltimore Album quilts hung in grand display. "The colors are gorgeous." Her exclamation of delight was lost on the burly guard who stood stone-faced at the door. Together with her sister-in-law, Betty, Diane approached the first magnificent quilt.

"Look at the amount of tiny, close stitching." As Diane leaned nearer to examine the craftsmanship, a loud buzzer rang. Startled, Diane jumped back and looked at the guard who was glaring at her.

"Imagine doing this intricate needlework without electric lighting," Diane commented as she read the date for the next quilt. Keeping her hands carefully behind her back so the guard would see she knew better than to touch the valuable collection, she moved closer to study the work. Another raucous buzz rang through the room.

"What was that?" Diane asked, bewildered. She noted the guard added a frown to his glare.

"Maybe the museum is testing a new burglar alarm. I don't think that guard likes us," Betty whispered as they moved on.

The women walked from one quilt to the next, awed by the workmanship and beauty. Over and over they were puzzled as the buzzer rang. The guard kept moving closer to them.

"I wish I had brought the magnifying glass I usually keep in my purse," Diane commented. "Then I could see the stitches even better." The buzzer blared again.

"I think I'm glad you didn't." Betty began to giggle. "I've figured it out. That alarm rings whenever you lean close to a quilt. The museum is protecting their treasures from damage. Can you imagine what it would sound like in here if you pulled out a magnifying glass? The guard would probably think you were going to catch the rays from the skylights and set the thing on fire."

Red-faced, Diane finished her tour of the quilts at a respectful, but visually frustrating, distance.

The world offers many attractive or exciting sights and activities, including an afternoon enjoying a quilt collection. Sometimes the activities are good but provide an undesirable distraction from more important pursuits. Some pleasures are actually harmful for us. Leaning too close to these temptations will endanger us. God wants to protect us from damage more than any museum wants to protect its quilt collection. When we throw ourselves into busy days with too much hustle and bustle, our time with God becomes crowded out. That communication with God is what keeps us alert to His warning buzzer.

GOD'S PATTERN
God's warnings often come in quiet thoughts.
We must listen to hear them above
the clamor of our day.

MAGIC QUILTS

He is despised and rejected of men;
a man of sorrows, and acquainted with grief:
and we hid as it were our faces from him;
he was despised, and we esteemed him not.
ISAIAH 53:3 KJV

C amp Magic, the name's a joke! I don't see the magic of sitting around a campfire crying about our son. I must have been insane when I let you talk me into coming this week." Chad's jaw muscles tightened as he struggled to stuff down his emotions.

"Give it a chance." Jeanne wiped her eyes with an already damp tissue.

"No chance of letting this program turn me into a blubbering mess like you and these other people. No way! I didn't even know these kids they lost, and nothing we do here can bring a single child back to life. Our Chuck is gone, and we just have to go on."

"We can go on as if we're really living if we let ourselves find healthy ways to express our grief." Jeanne's voice dropped to a whisper of despair at the frozen expression on her husband's face.

She smiled in gratitude when Grant, a burly construction worker, grabbed Chad's arm after lunch and propelled him over to the horseshoe pit.

Moist with perspiration, Chad joined her later in the lodge for the afternoon program.

"Grant's boy was the same age as ours when he died. It was an auto accident," Chad informed her as he sat down at a long table. Each couple was handed a muslin square and given instructions to paint a picture that reminded them of their deceased child. As Chad snorted and flung the material at his wife, Grant slid into a chair beside him.

"I wonder if we'll make a quilt out of our pictures like we did last year." Grant pointed to a comforter hanging at one end of the lodge. "My square is the one with the tent on it. Brad would jump up and down with excitement when I'd set it up in the backyard. The memories were so painful; I thought I'd die painting that picture. But, you know, afterward when I told last year's group why the tent represented a piece of Brad's life, the memory made me feel better. Whenever I volunteer at the counseling office and see my square hanging there, I remember the happy times with my son and the healing deepens.

"This year I want to paint a tricycle. Brad loved charging up and down the driveway on his red trike. I'm not much good at drawing. Since you're an engineer, do you think you could help me sketch a tricycle on this?" He tossed his material in front of Chad.

After he'd penciled in a trike for Grant, Chad turned to Jeanne. "Do you think a red wagon would represent our good times with Chuckie?"

Jeanne blinked back her tears. "Oh, Chad, it helps me so much to hear that you remember them."

"I know. I guess I thought if I didn't talk about him, somehow I could avoid dealing with the pain of his death. Maybe this quilt is magic after all," Chad mumbled into Jeanne's hair.

Our Lord understands our grief. He knows the depth of pain we experience when we suffer any kind of loss. Since He is always with us, we are never alone in our sorrow. Meeting with others who have experienced the same kind of grief helps us cope. When we fellowship with people who have suffered loss, the fact that someone else can still enjoy life after a tragedy encourages and strengthens us to rise above the suffering.

GOD'S PATTERN
God allows us to help others
in the same way He helped us
when we were in sorrow.

HOMESICK

O God, thou art my God; early
will I seek thee: my soul thirsteth for thee,
my flesh longeth for thee in a dry and
thirsty land, where no water is.
PSALM 63:1 KJV

"Bet you can't guess what I brought you from town," Bart called to Carrie, who stood in their shanty doorway. He pulled his team of horses to a stop in front of the water trough before he slid off the wagon seat. While the horses slurped the water, he strode to the shanty door, keeping one arm behind his back.

"Is it a licorice stick?" Carrie threw her arms around her husband's neck. "You didn't have to bring me anything. I'm just glad you're home. It's so lonely when you are gone. Not another soul to talk to. I started talking to the pigs."

"I know it's lonely out here." Bart stroked her hair. "Maybe next time I won't have to detour and hunt for missing cattle, then I'll take you to town with me when I go for supplies. Believe me. You were more comfortable here in the shade of our home." He wiped the sweat from his forehead with his sleeve, bringing his other arm around into view.

"A package!" Carrie squealed with delight.

"Hey, the pigs do talk to you." Bart laughed when the animals set up an answering commotion in their pen. "The postmaster said it arrived a week ago, but nobody was riding down this way."

Bart handed her the package and, putting an arm around her waist, ducked under the lintel of the doorway.

She carefully untied the string and unfolded the brown wrapping paper, smoothing it for future use as she went. "Look! A letter from Ma and one from Elsie." She set them aside to unwrap another packet. "Fabric scraps." Carrie's voice rose with excitement. "This must be a piece from Elsie's wedding gown." She held up a large swatch of delicate lawn fabric, dotted with tiny pink rosebuds. A sketch of her sister's dress was pinned to the material. "This is the next best thing to seeing her wear it." She blinked back tears as she examined the drawing. "These pleats would have emphasized Elsie's tiny waist. Oh, Bart can you picture what a beautiful bride she was?"

She pulled out a piece of pink cotton with a lilac print. Next, she found a sturdy chunk of light blue gingham. She read the note pinned to it: "'This was the backing the neighbors used when they quilted Elsie's wedding comforter.'"

"With these scraps I'll have enough material to complete my basket quilt top next winter when the weather traps us inside. Instead of feeling sorry for myself, I'll spend days quilting and thinking about my sister and how happy she must be as a new bride. Only this morning I asked for God's help to endure the winter."

"Don't forget I'm here with you." Bart nuzzled her hair and pulled a licorice stick out of his shirt pocket.

"And you do know how to sweeten the environment." Carrie took the candy and offered her lips in a kiss of thanks.

In the days before photographs were common, women sent clothing scraps as a form of information and a way to keep family ties strong. The pioneer women who settled our West experienced a "dry and thirsty land" in both their physical environment and their isolation from others and separation from loved ones. Clinging to God was the pathway to maintaining emotional health in difficult situations, as it is today. "For he satisfies the thirsty and fills the hungry with good things" (Psalm 107:9 NIV).

GOD'S PATTERN
He is faithful to supply a spiritual feast
to help us in our places of isolation.

COMPLETE JOY

Fulfil ye my joy, that ye be likeminded,
having the same love, being of one accord,
of one mind.
PHILIPPIANS 2:2 KJV

Nancy's excitement grew with each package the mailman brought to her door. Several months earlier she suggested an ambitious project to her college friends now graduated and scattered to their individual lives. The group of girls had developed close friendships during their enrollment at Virginia Tech. For four years, they lived, played, and studied together. Their many opportunities to unite in worship seemed to cement their friendships more than any other activity.

Now, Susan, Nancy's college roommate, was planning her wedding. As a gift suggestion, Nancy asked each of the friends to make a quilt square that represented an aspect of their campus life together. Nancy undertook the job of putting the pieces together and doing the final quilting for the present. Every arrival of a finished contribution in the mail brought a smile. Nancy relished the creativity of her chums. One cross-stitched a map of Virginia and highlighted the location of the campus, every girl's hometown, and the bride's and groom's birthplaces. The square stenciled with penguins brought a giggle and an almost forgotten memory of the bride's affection for the funny-looking birds. One of the patches was appliquéd with symbols of teaching since Susan studied for that profession. The squares represented a nice selection of crafts. In addition to the appliqué, cross-stitch, and stenciling, there was candlewicking and freehand painting with appropriate sayings stitched upon them.

Nancy alternated the four-cornered fabric with heart appliqués of a pink printed fabric to create a cohesive design. For Nancy, the time she spent putting the finished quilt pieces together revived pleasant memories. She relished the love poured into each square as evidenced by the care taken for each design. The classmates were still "all in one accord" giving time and thought to make something that would bless their friend. The joys of friendship and shared activities, dreams, hopes, giggles, and tears were resurrected in the quilt.

As the deadline drew near, the pressure mounted, but the work remained a complete joy. Knowing her friends' eagerness to continue their friendship, in spite of separation, made the stitching worthwhile.

More than material possessions or even exciting experiences, our relationships bring us the most joy in life. Maintaining friendships requires effort. Relationships are cemented by shared experiences, laughter, dreams, and thoughts. The greatest joy of all comes from our relationship with God. Fellowship with God offers the highest kind of joy available to us on this earth. As human friendships are birthed with the investment of our time, energy, and thought, we develop our friendship with God in the same way. Find time to converse with our heavenly Father. Delve into His love letter to us, the Bible. Develop the habit of listening for His voice with your heart.

GOD'S PATTERN

When we share our hopes and dreams
with our heavenly Father,
and cement our friendship with God by
making time for Him in our daily lives,
He will stitch joy into our lives.

HEAR MY CRY

A thousand shall fall at thy side,
and ten thousand at thy right hand;
but it shall not come nigh thee.
PSALM 91:7 KJV

I t's a hideous war." Tina's needle paused over the pink and gray tulip she was stitching to her muslin background. She sat with her mother close to the fireplace.

Her mother picked up a pile of pink flower petals cut from worn-out curtains. "I agree. All war is hideous, so why are you using your brother's confederate army uniform in your quilt?" She shuddered. "It's a gruesome reminder of the nurses cutting it off of him when he was wounded."

"I don't think of Robert; I think about Jim when I see the gray. I remember how handsome he looked in his uniform as he marched away to battle." Her vision blurred, and her stitching paused. "To think Jim and I would be married next month if he wasn't rotting away in a Yankee prison up north." She wiped her eyes. "When will this miserable war ever end? You'd think they could let a man go to get married," she said, poking her needle through the material with an angry stab.

"They don't want Jim shooting at them again, sis. Be glad he's not crippled." Tina turned at Robert's voice. With only a remnant of a limp, he had abandoned his cane, eager to rejoin the Southern forces.

She was thankful for Robert's recovery, and she thanked God every day for keeping Jim from permanent harm in the battle. But she hated the feeling that her life had halted in the middle of a sentence, as if every part of her life was holding its breath waiting for Jim to return, waiting for the war to end before motion would return to her world. She stitched faster on the quilt top. Her lips moved in quiet prayer for Jim's safety. As she stitched and prayed, the peace of God stole into her heart.

"I know what Bible verse I'm going to embroider on this quilt," Tina told her brother. "The one that tells us a thousand may fall on your left or right, but you will not fall. I think it's Psalm 91. Making this quilt is keeping me from going absolutely mad with worry about Jim."

Many quilts are preserved in collections bearing silent witness to the timeless occupation of women who, through their needles, expressed their fears and love for their sweethearts, husbands, and brothers caught up in the destructive forces of war. Quilts made during the Revolutionary War, the Civil War, the War of 1812, as well as World War I and World War II hang in museums to remind us of the human cost of our nation's freedom. Patterns of eagles, symbols of the United States, and names of soldiers were blended with scripture verses as women implored God for the safety of their loved ones.

Throughout the history of North America, women have drawn strength to endure separation, danger, and fears by studying the Bible and grasping the comfort of the God we learn about from it.

GOD'S PATTERN

None of our heartaches take God by surprise.
He knows when and how much help
to send us in our times of trouble.

Mile after Mile

Know ye not that they
which run in a race run all,
but one receiveth the prize?
So run, that ye may obtain.
1 CORINTHIANS 9:24 KJV

John blinked his eyes and slapped his thighs. His horse jerked to the right, breaking his steady pace. "Good boy. Wake me up a little. I don't want to fall asleep and tumble out of the saddle."

John didn't relish the hundred-mile ride from his homestead into town so soon after his last trip for supplies. He swatted flies with his hat before wiping the perspiration from his forehead. Days of travel through miles of woods alternating with meadows heated by the midsummer sun stood between him and the general store in Junaue County, Illinois. He patted his horse's neck as he spoke. "Someday this land will bustle with people, then you and I will have a less monotonous ride into town. We'll probably have some other towns a whole lot closer to our stake."

When at last the wood frame stores loomed into view on the horizon, John straightened in the saddle and went over his shopping list in his mind. He pulled to a stop in front of the general store and tied the reins to the rail.

"Need nails or tools already?" The storekeeper looked surprised to see John.

"I'll get some nails later, Stefan," John told the storekeeper.

"Need to look at your calico bolts first off. That's the main reason I made the trip so soon. Need to keep the little woman happy, you know." Feeling like the proverbial bull in a china closet, he fingered the material. "Wish I could have brought Ellie, but she's too near her time to jostle a hundred miles on a horse. She'd know better which colors go with what. That's a pretty pink flower on that cloth. Do you think it would blend with this purple stuff in a quilt?" He fished in a pocket and brought out a four-inch swatch of a lavender print.

"Ha!" Stefan laid the bolt on the counter. "Ask me about galvanized tin and things like that. I don't know anything about matching up colors. Let me see if Maizy can step away from her bread-making long enough to help." In a moment, Maizy followed Stefan from the family quarters behind the store, wiping the flour off her hands onto her apron.

"Ellie wants to finish this quilt she's making before the baby comes, but she had her heart set on making a border that matches all the way around instead of patching scraps together." John ducked his head. "Things like that get kinda important to a woman, you know, all alone out there with a first baby coming."

"I know." The wail of an infant penetrated the partition behind the counter. "This green print is soft, and it won't matter if the baby is a boy or a girl with lavender and green blended together." Maizy pulled a length off the bolt and set John's scrap on top of it. "Mighty nice of you to make the trip just for calico for Ellie." She patted John's arm.

"Now don't be saying I came all the way to town just for cloth." John shifted, and red began to rise from his collar and cover his face. "We can use some sugar and some of those nails Stefan mentioned."

"You must be swinging your hammer all day long if you already used up the nails I sold you last time." Stefan couldn't resist the jab at his friend.

"Getting ready for another mouth in the house, you know." John paid for his purchases and hurried to his horse before he took any more joshing about making a long journey for quilting cloth. John hardly noticed when the sun succumbed to clouds and sprinkles of rain cooled the land. Instead he pictured his Ellie, her hair tied back with a ribbon, opening the package of pale green calico.

It was common in pioneering days for the early settlers pushing toward the West to need to travel long miles to secure any supplies. Pretty new fabric was a luxury many women did not have. More than one pioneer man plied his way over tedious miles to bring his wife such a prize.

Sometimes the race God sets before us in life is quick and fascinating. Sometimes it is slow and monotonous. Either way, if we set our minds to obey God and do what He desires of us, there is a prize at the end of the race. When weariness tempts us to quit, we focus our minds on our love for God. The strength to finish comes from God Himself. The desire to please God motivates us to continue our efforts.

GOD'S PATTERN
God rewards our perseverance.
He calls us to the race;
He equips us to do it well;
and then He rewards us for doing it.

SOURCE OF POWER

"Don't be alarmed," he said.
"You are looking for Jesus the Nazarene,
who was crucified. He has risen! He is not here.
See the place where they laid him."
MARK 16:6 NIV

Kim shuddered when she looked at the wall hangings that hung in the museum. Centuries old, the pictures made by the Fon people of West Africa didn't make her think of feeling safe and cozy wrapped up in a quilt in front of a warm fireplace. The appliquéd pictures represented the violence of battle scenes. The works bristled with weapons in the hands of broad, angry-looking men.

Kim drew back at a grisly picture of an execution. Hardly what she'd choose to hang in her house, although the bright colors were pleasing from a distance. A sign told Kim the pieces were not made by women busy nurturing their young. Only men from the court tailors' guild of Fon, West Africa, made these pictures. This art form came from warriors making hangings to proclaim their power and authority. In their culture, winning wars was highly valued. The wall hangings were symbols of power. The irregular, asymmetrical designs also sported many brightly colored animals intended to convey the wealth of the warrior. The men who translated triumphant war stories into appliquéd wall hangings enjoyed important status in their society.

Even as Kim stood grimacing at the needlework, she realized

a battle raged for power and authority in her own life. Week after week she struggled to write reports for her bosses that pictured her as winning whatever the current contract required. While she didn't write about executing her competition, she did cut them down to picture herself as a victor. Reports that slandered others made her company's division look good.

The picture of Christ hanging on the cross came to her mind. He had chosen an infamous death so she could live. Then He conquered death and rose again. Right there in the museum, Kim breathed a prayer of surrender to God. If He could die and rise again for her salvation, His resurrected life could flow through her to help her at her work. She did not need to disparage others to come out ahead. She needed to ask for His power to perform her tasks. She determined to rely on His strength instead of her own.

∽

GOD'S PATTERN

Contrary to the instinct of man to maintain authority by
demonstrating power to our adversaries,
Christ died and, to man's surprise, arose again.
His death brought victory over His enemy and ours.

"The LORD shall fight for you, and ye shall hold your peace."
Exodus 14:14 KJV

The NIV translation reads: "The LORD will fight for you;
you need only to be still." When we still our hearts before God,
He will fight for us.

WHEN PUSH
COMES TO SHOVE

Yea doubtless,
and I count all things but loss for
the excellency of the knowledge of
Christ Jesus my Lord:
for whom I have suffered the loss of all things,
and do count them but dung,
that I may win Christ.
PHILIPPIANS 3:8 KJV

Ouch." Twelve-year-old Debbie jerked her left hand out from under the quilt she was working on. "I keep sticking my finger when I push the needle up from underneath the way you showed me. I hate this. It's no fun."

"A few finger pricks go with quilting. You said you like my quilt," Mother paused and held up her own nearly finished wall hanging, "and you'll like yours, too, when you see a little more progress. The sunbonnet is a simple pattern for a beginner. You're the one who asked to learn, remember?"

"I didn't know it meant poking myself to death." Debbie sucked her third finger. "Look, it's bleeding. Now I'll get blood all over my sunbonnet girl."

"Quilting requires a little practice, just like any other skill we try to master. Here, let's put a bandage on your finger." Mother wrapped the adhesive around Debbie's finger. "It'll help two ways—stop the bleeding and give you a little cushion in case the needle finds your finger again when you push the fabric up to make a tiny stitch. Eventually quilters get a callus on the finger they work with underneath the quilt. Look at me." Mother held her left hand up to Debbie's face. "See how tough the skin is on the one I use to put the pressure on the quilt? But the pressure is part of the reason I won the quilt prize at the county fair. Pressure helps me make tiny stitches. Look. I can get six to ten stitches every inch."

"Who cares?" Debbie frowned.

"It never hurts to strive for excellence. You don't need to be perfect, but you can keep pressing yourself to improve."

"Just let me do it the easy way. I get tired of pressure. It never stops at school. Somebody is always making fun of me when I try to act like a Christian. Anna made fun of me today because I chose Cindy to play on our softball team. She isn't as good as the others, but I felt sorry for her and didn't want to leave her out. Anna said she'd quit the team and join another one if I kept Cindy. If Anna quits, we'll lose every game because she's the star player."

"Sounds to me like you are letting the pressure make an excellent Christian out of you. I'll bet Anna's words pricked as badly as your needle did."

"Made me mad, but I don't care if we do lose. I don't want to hurt my friend's feelings."

"That's the way. Allow God to use the pressure to make you into a beautiful Christian." Mother hugged Debbie. "Loyalty to a friend is a whole lot more important than making a beautiful quilt. Maybe Cindy will take an interest in Jesus the next time you talk about Him."

When the pressures of life create heavy burdens and the pricks of a cruel world leave us stinging, we can turn to God and ask Him to help us grow under the press of our trials. He knows just how much pressure to allow into our lives. God's workmanship in us causes our lives to bless others and attracts them to our Savior. "But the God of all grace, who hath called us unto his eternal glory by Christ Jesus, after that ye have suffered a while, make you perfect, stablish, strengthen, settle you" (1 Peter 5:10 KJV).

GOD'S PATTERN

When we turn to God in the midst of suffering,
He strengthens us.
A settled peace is one pattern God stitches
into our lives when we turn to Him
for the strength to survive the pressures of living.

PAYING THE PRICE

Verily, verily, I say unto you,
Except a corn of wheat fall into the ground and die,
it abideth alone:
but if it die, it bringeth forth much fruit.
JOHN 12:24 KJV

The Revolution was far from Jane McCrea's mind early Sunday morning in July 1777 when she ran the brush through her thick, long hair one last time before picking up a bucket and heading for the gate of Fort Edward, New York. Excitement brought a bounce to her step and a lilt to her voice as she greeted a fort guard.

With the water she would fetch from the spring, she planned to freshen herself and fix breakfast. She had looked forward to this day when she would wed her handsome British lieutenant and become Mrs. David Jones. Her wedding thoughts interfered with her accustomed alertness when she was outside of the strong fort walls. In an instant her shivers of delight turned into a tremble of terror when a small group of Indians leaped from the brush at the spring.

The last sight Jane saw on what was supposed to be her wedding day was an Indian's sweaty arm held high above his dark scowl. His tomahawk swiftly descended to separate her lush, lovely hair from her vibrant head and transport her quickly to Christ her heavenly bridegroom instead of her earthly one.

His wedding so dominated Lieutenant David Jones's thoughts that morning when he reported to British General

John Burgoyne, he found it hard to concentrate on business. Even the arrival of a band of Indians failed to gain his attention until the leader of the group threw a scalp on Burgoyne's floor.

"Aha," the general reached into his camp desk and handed the Indian some silver coins, commenting that this would help discourage the citizens from supporting the revolutionary cause.

For a long moment, David Jones stood transfixed. He had run his fingers through Jane's thick flowing hair too often not to recognize the scalp belonging to his beloved. He turned on his heel and left the tent and the camp, hurrying toward the fort.

The news spread rapidly. Jane McCrea was killed on her wedding day. General Burgoyne was buying scalps to weaken his opposition. He thought the people would see they needed the British and stop rebelling against England. The reaction of the people was the opposite of what the general expected. Thousands of horrified men volunteered to join the colonial ranks. The colonial forces, weak in number and poor in supplies, suddenly swelled to numbers made formidable by determination born of outrage. Even Burgoyne's followers faltered in support of him. He met military defeat at nearby Saratoga; and, two months later when he surrendered, many taunted him by chanting Jane McCrea's name. Newspaper articles decried his actions, songs were sung heralding Jane as a heroine of the revolution, paintings were displayed, and the colonists rallied to what they perceived to be a righteous cause.

Many quilts are inspired by heroes and heroines. One depicting scenes from Jane's life on the front and with her story written on the back won a prize at a quilting show held in Williamsburg, Virginia, in 1997. The depth of emotion in the story as well as the quality of the work stopped every passerby.

The outrageous loss of Jane McCrea's life on a day meant for blissful joy fills us with regret. Who could have guessed that

God would take this terrible tragedy and use it as the turning point to help colonial America establish independence from England.

GOD'S PATTERN

Many times we are confused by
the turbulence of our lives,
but God sees beyond our limited understanding and
knows what serves His best and highest purposes.
"And we know that all things work together
for good to them that love God,
to them who are the called according to his purpose."
ROMANS 8:28 KJV

SWEET MEMORIES

He hath made his wonderful works to be remembered:
the LORD is gracious and full of compassion.
PSALM 111:4 KJV

Grandma, we have the best present. It's—" Four-year-old Kaitlyn squirmed when her mother clapped a hand over her mouth, stopping her eager disclosure before she ran up the steps into her grandparents' house.

"Don't tell the secret, Kaitlyn. You don't want to spoil the surprise. We have to wait until all the aunts, uncles, and cousins arrive before we give Grandma and Grandpa their anniversary present. Here, carry the rolls in." Noreen handed the bag to her daughter in a vain effort to distract her.

"You can't guess what we're bringing, Grandma." Kaitlyn pointed to the bulky package her father carried into the house and deposited on the coffee table.

"Whatever could be so big it needed yards of pretty gift paper to wrap it?" Grandma's eyes twinkled at Kaitlyn.

"We all look pretty on—"

"Kaitlyn, go play with Casey before you give the whole thing away." Noreen took Kaitlyn by the shoulder and steered her into the family room where her cousin, Casey, held out a doll to her.

"Here, dress your doll up for Grandma's anniversary party." Satisfied her daughter was safely distracted from blabbing about the family gift, Noreen returned to the car to unload her portion of the festive dinner the Brandts' four daughters had prepared for their parents' fiftieth anniversary.

Even Noreen fidgeted with anticipation long before the last van drove up to unload the final group of the family. "Let's give them the present before we eat," she whispered to her sister as she helped her unload the car and shepherd the children inside to join their cousins. "I don't think I can keep Kaitlyn from spilling the beans for a whole meal."

The family gathered with cameras in hand while the honored couple sat on the sofa and began to carefully peel away the tape from the package.

"You're too slow." Kaitlyn reached out an eager hand to help. "Tear it, Grandpa."

After a satisfying rip, a unique gift of love lay on the Brandts' laps. Murmurs of delight filled the room. Photographs of each family member were photocopied onto fabric squares and then combined to make a quilt commemorating the entire span of the Brandts' marriage. Grandma and Grandpa held up the large quilt filled with pictures of the most important treasures of their lifetime: their offspring. In the center was a reproduction of their wedding picture from fifty years ago. Around the center, every child was represented on the quilt by more than one picture, ranging from their babyhood to adulthood. The grandchildren also were represented in their various stages of growth.

Cameras clicked to record the surprise; and, moments later, they recorded the tears of joy coursing down the Brandts' faces. Sniffling, Noreen passed around a box of tissue. "Don't cry on the quilt. After all, it's an heirloom."

Before the small children could ask why everyone was crying about the perfect present, joyful voices filled the room with sometimes humorous, sometimes poignant stories as one after another, the family recalled memories triggered by the quilt of pictures.

Happy memories warm our hearts as thoroughly as quilts warm our bodies from the chill of a winter evening. Remembering the blessings God has poured into our lives revitalizes our faith and bolsters our joy. Make a conscious effort to stay grateful to God, not only because of what He has done for us, but because He is perfect and pure. Our faith grows when we remember His graciousness toward us.

GOD'S PATTERN

God's compassion is endless in our lives.
He builds joy into our hearts when
we remember His goodness.

DOWN IN THE DUMPS

Who redeemeth thy life from destruction;
who crowneth thee with lovingkindness
and tender mercies.
PSALM 103:4 KJV

Sherry put on rubber gloves and headed out the back door to the Dumpster between her yard and the shirt factory behind her house. She carried an empty shopping bag over her arm, a broomstick in one hand, and a kitchen stool in the other one.

"Let's see what treasures I find today," she told the calico cat who ran out to greet her when she plopped her chrome stool against the blue side of the Dumpster. The cat purred, rubbing her orange fur against her ankles. She leaned the broomstick against the Dumpster, pulled a chicken bone wrapped in aluminum foil out of her pocket, and placed it on the ground for the animal.

"You and I have a lot in common, Callie." Sherry scratched the cat's ears before she climbed on the stool and peered into the Dumpster. "We both scrounge around for scraps to make ends meet. The mortgage company, however, isn't likely to throw *me* a bone.

"Ah, looks like the good old shirt factory has several nice bones for me today." Sherry lifted a large piece of material out with her broomstick. "It's the perfect red to back my pinwheel top." Callie meowed as if to rejoice with her. "I've a customer willing to pay good money when I finish the pinwheel quilt."

She held it up to the light. "Callie, can you understand why they threw away a piece big enough to make shirts for an entire ball team? I wouldn't think this funny yellow line down the side is reason enough. Goodness, any self-respecting seamstress could cut that away and use the rest. The dried soda pop will wash out fine." She folded the fabric and tucked it into her shopping bag.

In response, the stray cat growled over its bone. "You'll have to wait until tomorrow for the other chicken leg. Sorry, it's just one scrap at a time from my table."

But the Dumpster yielded a better return. She stirred at the piles of scraps, discarded cardboard, and empty plastic bottles with her broomstick. "A perfect baby blue check." She lifted the material up on her broomstick. "I'll use this for the new baby line I'm making for the consignment store."

Callie purred. "You're right about that." Sherry nodded to the cat. "Pretty good pickings today."

Sherry snared some smaller brown and yellow scraps on her broom and shook them off into her bag. "Good for my flying geese pattern." She retrieved a few more pieces of solid blues before climbing down. "If it doesn't rain and the garbage pickup doesn't come extra early, I'll come back and sift through the bin again tomorrow and bring you the other bone. Gracious, I might celebrate tonight by eating some extra chicken and bring you the wishbone tomorrow.

"Some folks might not like the view of this big old Dumpster in their backyard, but the good Lord put it here for me."

Sherry patted the cat one more time, then picked up the kitchen stool and walked to her back door. She gave a satisfied wave of her hand to the cat and went straight to her sewing machine to make as much progress on her quilts as she could in the remaining daylight.

When we feel down in the dumps, God has the means and

the desire to rescue us. Whether it is in an unorthodox manner like Sherry, maintaining the supplies for her quilting business from the throwaways of a shirt factory, or a more standard route to provision, God provides our needs. When we turn to Him, He also supplies us with emotional insights to improve our lives.

GOD'S PATTERN
He takes the refuse of our lives
and forms it into a useful pattern
that accomplishes valuable results.

A GORGEOUS SIGHT

And let the beauty of the LORD our God be upon us:
and establish thou the work of our hands upon us;
yea, the work of our hands establish thou it.
PSALM 90:17 KJV

Rosemarie could hardly take in the beauty of the quilt. She wouldn't argue with the judges who hung a large blue first-place ribbon prominently above the breathtaking work. A flourishing flower garden filled the wall hanging. Hundreds of flowers fashioned from tiny bits of fabric splashed across the width of the quilt. Each flower was identifiable and contained two or more colors that combined to make the flower appear almost real.

Awed by the intricate work, Rosemarie wondered how many hours it took to piece together such a masterpiece. The craftsmanship and artistry of the piece before her made her own quilt tops look like the work of a kindergarten student. Even the garden wall was sewn with each brick individually fashioned and nestled close to the next one. Subtle color changes brought depth as the wall curved away. The breathtaking beauty lifted her mind off of her trials for the moment.

Beauty does that. It offers a tiny respite of pleasure in the midst of life's difficulties. It's never a waste of time to acquire the skills required to create a splash of beauty in a world full of trouble and evil. Beauty is the nature of God Himself. A lovely creation in any artistic form reminds us of the God who created the ones who perform the artwork. While Rosemarie looked at the magnificent creativity of a woman who was only a name on a quilt show label, she thought about the creativity of her Lord, who was the ultimate Master craftsman of her life and of all the lives of her loved ones.

When Rosemarie came to the quilt show, her heart felt heavy with concern over her five-month-old grandson who lay in a hospital, fighting for his life. If God Almighty could inspire and enable a woman to create such a gorgeous sight as the quilt that hung before her, He could inspire and enable the doctors and nurses who were searching for causes and cures to restore her grandson's health.

Beauty inspires us to look more closely at the God we love. Seeing the beauty of God helps us better understand the depth and breadth of His love. The more we know God, the more we see His beauty and the beauty He creates in our lives even in the midst of troubles we do not understand. We come to appreciate God for Himself, beyond what He does for us. Psalm 27:4 (KJV) tells us: "One thing have I desired of the LORD, that will I seek after; that I may dwell in the house of the LORD all the days of my life, to behold the beauty of the LORD, and to inquire in his temple."

GOD'S PATTERN
When we recognize God is the creator of beauty,
we understand the source of our own creativity.
Ecclesiastes 3:11 (NIV) tells us:
"He has made everything beautiful in its time.
He has also set eternity in the hearts of men;
yet they cannot fathom what God
has done from beginning to end."

THE SUBSTITUTE

But God commendeth his love
toward us, in that,
while we were yet sinners,
Christ died for us.
ROMANS 5:8 KJV

D id you make this quilt?"
Ruth smiled when she answered. "No, my friend Jill made it."

"Tell Jill it's a beautiful work of art," the lady in the blue suit said. "I love lots of roses on comforters." She leaned closer to look at the stitches. "Your friend did a lovely job."

"If you'll let me take your picture, you can help me tell Jill." Ruth laid down her pad on which she had written the woman's comments and picked up a camera. "My friend is in the hospital recovering from surgery for cancer. She's so disappointed she can't be here. I know she would enjoy the wonderful response her quilt is receiving at the quilt show. I'm standing in for her today and recording all the nice things people say and taking some pictures of people admiring her quilt so she will feel like she participated in the excitement, at least in a small way."

"How thoughtful." The lady squinted at Ruth's name tag. "Didn't I see a quilt with your name hanging in the exhibit?"

"Yes, but it's not nearly as exquisite as this one."

"People may be saying nice things about your quilt."

"Never mind. I really want to be here."

Over and over for the full three days of the quilt show,

Ruth wrote down the words of admiration people spoke when they looked at the rose quilt. Her camera recorded the moment when the judges hung an honorable mention on the piece. No one in her quilter's guild had ever won a ribbon at a show before.

When Ruth went to retrieve her own quilt at the end of the show, she was dumbfounded to find another honorable mention ribbon hanging by it. She didn't say a word about her own award when she took her notepad and pictures straight from a one-hour developing store to her friend's hospital bed.

"Look. You won a ribbon." Ruth pinned the yellow ribbon onto her friend's nightgown. "Everyone loved your quilt. Listen to the things people said." A big smile watered with tears decorated her friend's face while Ruth read page after page of enthusiastic praise for Jill's pretty comforter. Jill recognized lots of women from her quilt guild in the pictures, but she found great satisfaction in the number of strangers who complimented her quilt. They had no reason to make nice remarks about her work unless they genuinely admired it.

Ruth took her sick friend's place at the quilt show to allow her to participate in a small way. She willingly sacrificed enjoying the rewards of her own quilt. Because of her, Jill enjoyed some of the pleasures of a triumphant day. Jesus Christ took our place on the cross in order to allow us the privilege of entering into eternal life. His sacrifice was the ultimate one of substituting His life and blood for our sins.

GOD'S PATTERN

God designed a way for us to enjoy
the triumph of Jesus Christ over sin and death,
which allows us to live with Him forever and ever.

Hiding Place

Thou art my hiding place;
thou shalt preserve me from trouble;
thou shalt compass me about
with songs of deliverance. Selah.
Psalm 32:7 KJV

W ho's the man riding in front of those soldiers?" Calvin
asked his friend, Joseph Wadsworth, as they stood
together in front of the Hartford house of legislation in the
Connecticut colony.

"Bad news for freedom, that's who. He's Sir Edmund
Andros, whom King James II appointed governor over the
Dominion of New England." Joseph raised his chin and set his
jaw in a firm line. "Can't be in Connecticut's best interest for
him to arrive in town. In 1675 his troops came into Saybrook
and seized the fort.

"Thank God for feisty citizens loyal to the Connecticut
colony." The local schoolmaster pounded his right fist into his
left palm. "They put up such resistance, the troops rode out
again. Afraid of a little bleeding, I guess."

"Let's hope Connecticut doesn't shed any blood because of
this visit. We aren't going to stand for loss of freedom in 1687
any more than we did twelve years ago," Calvin said.

Later in the day, Calvin stood outside an open window and
listened to the hot words tumbling from the legislators' meeting
room.

"The charter represents our freedom. We will never surrender it."

"The king of England gave the charter to John Winthrop for the Connecticut Colony in 1662, and we won't give it up." Voices blended together in protest against Sir Edmund Andros.

Every time he heard Joseph's voice ring out for freedom, Calvin swelled with pride for his friend. The debate raged on until most of the listeners standing outside drifted home for a late dinner, but the passionate talk continued. Calvin hoped his wife would understand why he wanted to stay and listen. Their lifestyle was at stake.

When the light faded, the dissension did not. The men in the chamber lighted several candles so they could make notes and read the expressions on their fellow legislators' faces. Some of the men were ready to turn the charter over. Occasionally fingers reached for the document on the table as if to take possession of the paper for their point of view.

A strong gust of wind stormed up the street. It blew Calvin's hat off as it swept inside the room and extinguished the candles. As Calvin fumbled for his hat in the street, he felt someone brush past him. A moment later the candles were relit, and Sir Edmund Andros's bellow of rage pierced the air. The charter was gone.

Calvin turned and quickly followed the shadowy figure who had brushed past him to a nearby grove of large oak trees. Even in the dark, Calvin recognized the profile of Joseph Wadsworth. He was close enough to see his friend pull a paper from his coat and stuff it into a hole in a large oak tree. Sir Edmund Andros could not seize a paper that had disappeared.

One year later Sir Edmund Andros's rule ended when King James II lost power in England. Soon afterward, Calvin's wife, Dorcas, and other women began stitching a new quilting pattern of four green oak leaves arranged in a circle and connected by eight brown acorns. The women, who called the pattern the Charter Oak quilt, made it as a reminder of freedom in Connecticut.

God stands ready to protect us in times of danger. He knows the best way to hide us from trouble. Sometimes we aren't aware of the danger or His protection. In addition to hiding us from trouble with our earthly enemies, He defends us from the archenemy, Satan, who desires to destroy us. He also understands our need for emotional protection. We can ask Him to protect our lives in every realm—physical, emotional, and spiritual.

GOD'S PATTERN

God values our freedom to choose to follow after Him.
He allows us to decide how much we will trust Him.
He helps us grow strong enough to lean
on His divine wisdom instead of our feelings.

PURE LOVELINESS

*But as he which
hath called you is holy,
so be ye holy in all
manner of conversation.*
1 PETER 1:15 KJV

D id you hear what Ruby said about Liz yesterday?" Gertie
cupped her hand beside her mouth as she spoke.

"No, what?" Viva raised her head from her quilting.

"You won't believe me when you hear. It's a juicy story."
Gertie's eyes glinted with mischief.

Gertie leaned closer to Viva and lowered her voice. Instead
of going unnoticed by the members of the quilting group, the
furtive conversation drew attention. Needles stilled and all eyes
turned to Gertie. She straightened up in her seat as red crept
into her face.

"Tell us, too, Gertie. Must be some tale," Sable called out.

"Let's turn on some more lights in this room. I'm having
trouble seeing my work," said Beth, trying to change the
subject. "This white stitching on white material requires good
eyesight. Maybe my eyes are too old to attempt it."

"It's worth the effort. The serene elegance of pure white
creates a lovely quilt," Halley said, understanding what Beth
wanted to do.

"It reminds me of purity, which is why I chose it for a bridal
gift."

"Come on, Gertie, out with your story." Sable was not
distracted.

"Let's not," Beth said, keeping her voice calm. "Remember when we started meeting we determined to only speak well of one another."

"This isn't about us. It's someone else." Gertie tried to defend herself.

"I guess conversation is like your quilt, Beth; even a few stitches of another color would spoil the pure loveliness of the work," Halley spoke up, and, after an awkward pause, the conversation moved on to more uplifting topics.

Instead of listening to gossip about others, we can turn a conversation to a less destructive direction by changing the subject. When we refuse to listen to gossip, we become instruments God uses to demonstrate righteousness. Bringing Jesus into a conversation ushers His light into it since Jesus is the light of the world. Where His presence is, it becomes uncomfortable to gossip.

⌒

GOD'S PATTERN

Purity of conversation is God's design.
"Only let your conversation be
as it becometh the gospel of Christ:
that whether I come and see you,
or else be absent, I may hear of your affairs,
that ye stand fast in one spirit,
with one mind striving together
for the faith of the gospel."
PHILIPPIANS 1:27 KJV

BULLETPROOF VESTS

He shall cover thee with his feathers,
and under his wings shalt thou trust:
his truth shall be thy shield and buckler.
PSALM 91:4 KJV

As James packed a change of clothes in his saddlebag, ivory arms slid around his waist from behind. Dropping the bag, James smiled and grabbed Glenda's hands. Twisting around, he cupped her chin in his hand. "I'll miss you, my little poesy."

"Make haste and rout the Anglo-Saxons then hurry back to me safe and sound. My life holds still until you return." Glenda pursed her lips into a pout.

"We'll only find minor skirmishes on our foray. The Battle of Hastings won the big war for William the Conqueror. When we suppress these local rebellions, I'll have my steed at a gallop for you."

Glenda wrapped her arms around his neck. "Did you notice that my seamstress mended the tear your angry hound made in the quilted clothing? I can't help but wonder if a hound can cause a tear, what would a lance do when thrown from a racing steed? Will it protect your heart?"

"It's my skill which protects my skin, but the thick fabric takes the brunt of a glancing blow from a dagger or arrow." He kissed the tip of her nose. "I'm well motivated to dodge all the weapons and return. You've provided me with excellent protection with closely quilted, thick clothing."

Early in the history of warfare, man began searching for

techniques to improve their safety. The warriors of the eleventh century used quilted fabric as armor worn under their chain mail in an effort to provide some additional protection from the dangers of battle.

God provides His believers with a wrap of protection against the dangers of our battles, whether they are physical, spiritual, or emotional. The entire Ninety-first Psalm speaks of His protection for us. When we read about the protection of His feathers, we think of a mother hen's feathers. She clucks to call her chicks when she wants to hide them from danger under her wings. When we heed the call of God and run under His will, we experience His protection. God's protection is available to us when we run from the world's standards to hide ourselves under His love.

GOD'S PATTERN

When we align our choices with His will,
which we find in the scriptures,
God's technique is to wrap us in His protection.

HANDS ON

Though he fall, he shall not be utterly cast down:
for the LORD upholdeth him with his hand.
PSALM 37:24 KJV

I want yellow."

"I want mine blue."

"Will this paint wash off? Yuck. I don't want a green hand all summer."

"Is there enough red paint for my handprint?"

The kindergarten classroom buzzed with the excitement of five-year-old voices enthusiastic about their project to honor their teacher, Mrs. Mason. Since the teacher's baby was born two weeks early, she would miss the final weeks of school with her class. The room mothers took advantage of her absence to plan a surprise for the teacher who had won their admiration for her gentle and yet thorough preparation of her students for first grade.

"Can I put both hands on the quilt to show Mrs. Mason I love her?"

"Then I get to put my footprint on, too, because I love her that much."

The children responded with enthusiasm to the idea of making a quilt of their handprints for their teacher.

One by one, each child walked to the front of the class where their room mothers stood gripping eager wrists to control how much and where the paint landed. After pressing a handprint onto the large muslin piece stretched across several tables, the room mother kept a tight hold on the wiggly child until she dunked the paint-layered hands in a washbasin of sudsy water. Even with their best efforts, clothing and assorted classroom fixtures received unplanned decoration.

Before snack break, the material carried twenty colorful handprints, each one with a name scrawled underneath in childish handwriting.

"Tomorrow, when the paint is dry, you will each help with the sewing to make this top into a quilt," the substitute teacher promised before the children lined up to go home.

Before school the next day, busy mothers arranged the painted top over batting and a backing. Each child was allowed to choose a color of heavy yarn, and the mothers resisted the urge to laugh at the pursed lips, stuck-out tongues, and other grimaces the children made threading their blunt, big-eyed needles.

"Don't I sew good, teacher?" The curly blond girl beamed with pride when her stitch succeeded in going through all three layers and back up to the top where she tied a knot and cut the thread. She bit her tongue as she concentrated. The mothers' backs ached from a morning of bending over to help position stitches and determine if the needle went through all the layers, not to mention ensuring the scissors cut only thread, not material.

As a good teacher, Mrs. Mason had left her handprint on each child's life as she diligently prepared the students for their future schooling. Teachers, parents, and even people with only casual contact imprint our children's personalities and character, bringing some impact to the children's future decisions. When we are with children, we must bear in mind that our words and actions are placing a print on their lives as surely as if we put a paint-laden hand upon them. Children prosper with adults who take care to provide good influences in their lives.

GOD'S PATTERN

God holds us in His hand
and keeps His hand on us.
When praying for the children in our lives,
ask God to keep His hand
upon them to direct their ways.
Pray they don't fall away from God,
and ask Him to pick them up and
restore them when they do.
Be alert for the opportunities we have
to represent the hand of God and
influence little ones to believe in Him.
"And the hand of the Lord was with them:
and a great number believed,
and turned unto the Lord."
ACTS 11:21 KJV

WHERE'S HOME?

Thou wilt show me the path of life:
in thy presence is fulness of joy;
at thy right hand there are pleasures for evermore.
PSALM 16:11 KJV

I liked our house in Virginia better," Kara whined as the Johnsons' car stopped behind the moving van in the driveway of the family's new house.

"You'll have a bigger room all to yourself in this house." Mother kept her voice cheerful.

"I'll share a room with Kara if I can move back to Virginia. Texas doesn't have any trees. Virginia's better," Rachel agreed with her younger sister.

"The Air Force needs Daddy to live in San Antonio for a while. And there are too trees. There's one right in our front yard."

"Not lots of trees like Virginia." Kara stuffed her thumb in her mouth.

"We'll have fun finding out what fun things we can do in our new state." Loraine Johnson's patience was wearing thin.

"It's not fun if I can't play with Tammy." Rachel's pout matched Kara's. "She's not in Texas."

Mother sighed. "I know you miss your friend, but you'll meet some wonderful new ones here. Let's go inside and see if the movers have set up your beds."

"I'll get lost at night trying to find the bathroom," Kara complained as the girls trailed behind their mother up the stairs to find their father.

To Loraine's relief, the furniture in both the girls' rooms was in place. "Here's the box marked sheets and quilts," Loraine said. "Let's make your beds first thing."

The girls grabbed their quilts with glad cries when Mother pulled them from the carton.

Kara lay down on her bed after her mother spread the quilt over the clean sheets and smiled. "It's fun to be by myself," she said as her sister and mother stepped across the hall to make Rachel's bed.

"It feels like home now," Rachel said. "I love my doggy quilt."

Loraine Johnson sighed with relief at the difference in her girls' attitudes. They began to explore their new house with enthusiasm instead of complaints.

On future moves, the first item of business for this military family was to set up and make the girls' beds. Somehow the presence of their quilts on a familiar piece of furniture established security for the children and smoothed the way for adjustments.

When we sense God's presence in our lives, we enjoy a secure feeling and adjust to the changes life brings. Since change is one of the guarantees of life, we need to learn to find His presence and become comfortable in it. His presence helps us adjust to the unexpected.

<hr/>

GOD'S PATTERN

To maintain the flexibility we require in life,
we need to learn how to enjoy God's presence.
The time we spend in prayer, reading the Bible,
and meditating on the character of God
and His nature will help us feel at home
and comfortable in His presence
no matter how our surroundings change.

FREE INDEED

And ye shall know the truth,
and the truth shall make you free.
JOHN 8:32 KJV

Caroline slipped her handkerchief from her pocket. Turning her head, she dabbed at her eyes, hoping none of the women noticed. As she slid the hankie into her bodice, she looked around. Every head was down with each woman scrutinizing her own stitching. *This is the last time I try to work on Reggie's Freedom quilt in front of other people. I can't seem to help crying over it.* Caroline straightened her shoulders.

"Is this Reggie's Freedom quilt, Caroline?" Melody leaned over to examine the eagles marching around the edge of the blanket.

Caroline sighed. "It seems impossible, but he'll be twenty-one before the year is over. I want to finish his Freedom quilt for his birthday in November. How fast the years have flown."

"You have a lot of Bible verses on his quilt." Melody pointed to the one from Proverbs which warned young men to heed God's instruction.

"I keep thinking of important verses I want him to re-member as he makes the serious decisions of life. Now that he's grown, I can't follow him around and whisper good advice in his ear, but he'll take his quilt with him when he leaves home. Maybe it will remind him of his Christian heritage and keep him on the right path." Caroline clutched the quilt to her heart.

Melody sighed. "I can't imagine what I'll do when my Tommy leaves. In only ten years he'll be twenty-one."

"Make him a Freedom quilt when the time comes. The warmth it provides is probably less important than what making it does for a mother's peace of mind. I find myself praying the scriptures I embroider for him with stitches of love. By the time I finish making the comforter, I hope my heart understands what my mind already knows—Reggie is not my little boy any longer. He's a man. The Freedom quilt represents the gift of independence his father and I grant him on his twenty-first birthday."

"That sounds too final for me." Melody shook her head.

"Why do you think I have to stop so often and wipe away the tears?" Caroline pulled her hankie out again. "Until Reggie turns his own son loose someday, he won't appreciate how much of a sacrifice it is to let him go. Oh, he'll go on loving us. Maybe he'll come and ask advice sometimes, but it won't be the same as rocking away the hurts of a little boy, or dusting off grass and leaves from my skirt after a spontaneous hug." She finished embroidering the words "Holy Bible" on the front of the large black rectangle in the center of the quilt. "I'm letting him go, but I hope the quilt will remind him of what I taught him."

A custom for some women in the latter part of the nineteenth century and early twentieth century was to make a quilt for their sons' twenty-first birthday that acknowledged that the boy was now an independent man, free from the restraints of his mother. Judging from the amount of scripture used on some of these quilts, the mothers hoped their sons would use their independence to serve Christ.

Real freedom comes from allowing Christ to cleanse us from sin. The truth of the gospel provides a permanent source of liberating freedom. Some young adults think independence from the rules and expectations of parents or society provides liberty, but they later discover this freedom only leads to consequences they had not expected. The freedom that follows a clear conscience brings a liberty beyond the understanding of people without Christ.

GOD'S PATTERN
God intended the instructions of the Bible
to bring us the freedom of clean hearts instead of
blind bondage to a list of do's and don'ts.

I'll Cut the Sheet

I will not leave you comfortless:
I will come to you.
JOHN 14:18 KJV

The pressure of unshed tears behind Cheryl's eyes sent shooting stabs of pain through her sinuses as she adjusted the receiving blanket around her sleeping baby. With one finger, she traced the outline of one of the Raggedy Ann dolls decorating the flannel.

"Mama will make you a cake tomorrow for your first birthday," Cheryl whispered. "I'll make it in the shape of a doll just like the pictures on your blanket. Think how good the icing will taste." She listened to Brook's shallow breathing. "Can you hold on for one more day, precious girl?" She stroked her baby's cheek, searching for even a tiny trace of color in the pale face.

"I take that back." She cradled her daughter close. "You don't have to struggle to live anymore. I release you to God." Still, the tears didn't flow.

In the agony of the months that followed Brook's death, the gray-laden skies of winter matched the despair in her heart. "Even the clouds don't rain!" she shouted one time at the sky. Her grief seemed dammed up inside.

People tried to help, and Cheryl went through the motions of living. She bought groceries and cooked meals that tasted like sawdust. She accepted invitations for lunch and made polite noises in response to her friends' chatter. Everything she did was as if it were happening in a thick fog, a cloud of pain that hovered over her life. Nowhere did the sun shine in her soul.

"I've got to get on with my life." She watched her husband try to reach her and finally draw away from the rebuff of indifference. Only the pictures of Brook with her first birthday cake brought her any comfort. Brook had smiled at the bright colors and smacked her thin lips over tiny tastes of icing. Cheryl never regretted making the elaborate cake for her baby, although she was much too ill to eat it.

"Got a good idea," Cheryl's friend Dina announced, standing on her doorstep. "Put on your lipstick; we're going to visit the quilting guild that meets in my church every month."

"I don't quilt."

"Neither do I, but we both sewed layettes when our babies were coming. I'm guessing we might like quilting." Dina was persistent, and Cheryl's detached state made it easier to go along placidly with her friend's efforts to help.

The projects the women stitched at the meeting piqued her interest. When she watched the day's demonstration of appliqué, she grasped an idea. At home she rummaged through the box of baby things her husband had packed away until she found the Raggedy Ann receiving blanket. She laid out a length of muslin her friend provided and picked up a pair of scissors. After a moment's hesitation, she clenched her teeth and cut a slash into the flannel up to the closest Raggedy Ann picture. As she cut around the doll's edges, her vision blurred with a cascade of tears. She laid down the scissors and sobbed, releasing her grief in great torrents.

Over and over she repeated the process, cutting out a doll and then crying as if her heart would break. Instead of breaking, however, she began to feel a touch of healing. She ironed under the edges and, one by one, stitched the dolls onto her muslin.

Slowly, as the project progressed, smiles accompanied her stitching as often as tears. She began to recall the happy times with Brook: her first tooth, her giggles when Daddy tickled her, and the crooked smile over her first birthday cake.

"Your top's ready to quilt," the ladies at the quilting guild encouraged her, happy to see the luster restored in their friend's eye, and her enthusiasm for life returning. "What are you going to use for the backing?"

"I thought one of Brook's crib sheets would make a good backing."

"Perfect," Dina agreed.

At the next meeting, everyone was surprised to see Cheryl with a different project. "Did you finish your Raggedy Ann quilt?" Dina asked.

"No, I couldn't cut the sheet. I just couldn't."

The ladies changed the subject. Laughter bounced around the room as usual when the women gathered. At the end of the meeting, Cheryl, whose silence had lasted the entire meeting, spoke up. "Your friendships and quilting have helped me heal. I'm going to cut the sheet and finish my quilt. The Raggedy Ann pictures bring good memories. I want to see them hanging in my house."

God has a way to bring healing for the grief of each sorrow in our lives. He sent the Holy Spirit to bring us comfort. God understands the pain we experience in life, and His heart is touched by our sorrow.

∽

GOD'S PATTERN
He does not leave us alone in despair
but provides a way to healing.
The act of creating helps us tune into
our great Creator and open up for His comfort.

WHAT?

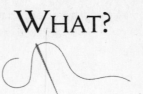

And he called his ten servants,
and delivered them ten pounds,
and said unto them, Occupy till I come.
LUKE 19:13 KJV

P lease, please, let me sew!" Jasmine tugged at her mother's arm.

"Let go, Jasmine. You're going to make my stitches crooked. After you turn seven, I'll let you sew. Right now I have the perfect job for a five-year-old. When the ladies go home from our quilting bee, you can pick up all the threads and little pieces of material that fall on the floor."

"That's no fun. Let me cut." Jasmine picked up a nearby pair of scissors and whacked the air, alarming the nearest lady who ducked out of the way.

"You have to be even older to do the cutting." Mother removed the scissors before her daughter could hurt someone with them. "If the pieces aren't cut exactly right, the pattern won't fit together correctly."

Soon Jasmine tired of watching the ladies and wandered off to play with her dolls.

Her interest in quilts was long forgotten by the time her mother called her to come help clean up.

"Please pick up all the trash and put it in here." Mother gave her a paper bag and pointed out the threads and scraps littering the floor under the quilting frame.

"I don't wanna. I wanna help make the pretty cover."

"Picking up these threads is the right size job for you. Look how hard it is for your big mama to crawl around under the frame." Mother dropped to her knees and demonstrated her tight fit underneath.

Jasmine laughed.

"See. Your fingers are just the right size to pick up the threads. My fingers are too big and have to try several times before I finally grab a thread."

Jasmine plucked up a thread.

"Good girl. Get your fingers trained for picking up, and you'll be ready to sew before you know it."

Jasmine's new job was to pick up, and pick up she did. It didn't take Jasmine long to figure out complaining wouldn't win her a reprieve. She eventually made it into a game by pretending she was a bird finding material to build a nest.

"Look, Jasmine, I bought you a printed quilt square to sew and learn to make even stitches." A brown bunny stood in the center of the material Mother gave her. Around the edges blue, yellow, and green shapes formed the borders. "You've been so good at the clean-up task, I believe you're ready for a more grown-up stage."

How many times do we fret over chores that seem insignificant to us? God is pleased when we accomplish the small jobs as well as the ones we deem important. What seems unimportant to us, God views as a stepping-stone of preparation for larger responsibility. In Matthew 25:21 (KJV) we read: "His lord said unto him, Well done, thou good and faithful servant: thou hast been faithful over a few things, I will make thee ruler over many things: enter thou into the joy of thy lord." In God's training program, the small acts come before the bigger things.

∽

GOD'S PATTERN

God wants us to fill our time with worthwhile activities that He directs. His plan is for us to occupy ourselves for the advancement of the kingdom.

A Cold, Dank Cell

"I needed clothes and you clothed me,
I was sick and you looked after me,
I was in prison and you came to visit me."
MATTHEW 25:36 NIV

L isten. I hear the jailer's keys rattling." When Mary pulled her tattered skirt down to cover herself, her listless baby squealed a few weak cries of protest at the loss of warmth the thin material offered.

"Maybe Mistress Fry comes with more help." Hope lifted the veil of indifference from Gilda's face.

"A sane lady wouldn't return ta this stinkin' rat hole if'n a body had any choice in da matter." Nelda rolled over on the bare floor, but the other woman fastened her eyes on the slit in the heavy wooden door.

Prisoners who languished in nineteenth-century England prisons lived in miserable squalor. In the unheated, dank cells, people seldom enjoyed even a thin smattering of dirty straw on the cold floors when they tried to sleep. Almost no one possessed any sort of covering for the cold nights. Most prisoners wore inadequate clothing. Elizabeth Fry, a Quaker, was a quilt maker in nineteenth-century England when she learned of the dreadful conditions women prisoners suffered in the Newgate Prison in London, England. Warmed by fluffy quilts on her own comfortable bed, she couldn't ignore her horrified reaction when she learned of the wretched conditions incarcerated women endured. Some women even bore babies while imprisoned and had no blankets to wrap them in or clothing to warm them.

Not a woman content to sit and talk, Elizabeth took it upon herself to help. The attitude of the day hindered her efforts because people often considered poverty the justified lot of the poor and thought they shouldn't tamper with their status. Society considered the terrible prison conditions as part of the punishment for crimes. Authorities tried to discourage Elizabeth. Armed guards avoided entering the cells because they considered the prisoners extremely dangerous.

In spite of the warnings, Elizabeth enlisted the aid of women who were members of the Society of Friends. Together they began the challenging task of improving the living conditions of women in prison. The cries of children cold and sick from exposure, the numbed stares of mothers, helpless and without hope, drove the Quaker women to persevere in spite of the obstacles.

Elizabeth persuaded women to donate pile after pile of fabric scraps for the sewing classes she set up for imprisoned women. In spite of the stench of the prison, she and her volunteers taught the women how to turn the material scraps into clothing and patchwork quilts to cover themselves in the cold. The gratitude of the women spurred the volunteers to increase their help and ignore any risk and discomfort.

When Elizabeth learned court judges often ordered women to travel by ship to penal colonies, she began to supply them with tea and other provisions for the long journey. She gave the women scraps for patchwork quilts that they made on the tedious voyage. Arriving at their destination without a penny, they could at least sell their quilts for a little money to improve their lot.

If we put our minds to it, God can give us creative ways to help others find a happier life. Elizabeth Fry not only offered help, she found a way to teach the women skills so they could help themselves in the future. Prisons still contain people in need of emotional soothing and comfort.

GOD'S PATTERN
By teaching others to sew and quilt,
we pass on an art form that allows
the person to become productive.
Since God never becomes discouraged
in offering us hope and help,
we can persist to offer the same to others.

OVER AND OVER

That the generation to come might know them,
even the children which should be born;
who should arise and declare them to their children.
PSALM 78:6 KJV

Alice snuggled under the quilt on the four-poster bed in her grandmother's guest room. She loved bedtime when she visited her grandparents. After a bedtime story and before the good night kisses, she and Grandma played a game with the Flower Garden quilt. Alice pointed at a little piece of fabric and asked, "Whose dress was this?"

Grandma answered by saying things like, "The tiny pink flower material came from your mother's dress for her first piano recital. The yellow material was from Aunt Jan's dress for her first dance."

Alice knew the answers by heart and didn't need to ask anymore, but she never tired of hearing Grandma describe each event the many dresses had starred in. After Grandma heard her prayers and kissed her good night, Grandma turned on the dim light of the milk glass hurricane lamp in the corner of the room, and Alice could continue to look at her grandmother's Flower Garden quilt. She rubbed her fingers around each medallion and remembered the stories about when her mother and Aunt Jan were little girls, and when Grandma wore a blue-striped dress on her honeymoon to go to the theater for the first time ever.

Wrapped in the quilt and warmed by cozy memories of her

heritage, Alice fell asleep planning for tomorrow.

Her tomorrows at Grandma's house were always fun. In the daytime the quilt served as a table for tea parties under the large oak tree, or the classroom where she taught her dolls their lessons, or the train of her gown when she played royal wedding.

Today the quilt is an important part of Alice's memories. She keeps it on her guest bed and can still recite the stories hidden in the pretty fabric of the quilt.

We become strong in God's principles the same way that Alice learned her heritage, by repetition. When we tell specific examples of when God blessed our family, we are preserving our children's spiritual heritage. The stories of the Lord's work in our lives improve our understanding of the kingdom of God. Because of the value of repetition, we read the same Bible over and over to grow and develop in understanding.

GOD'S PATTERN

Just as the repetition of a quilt pattern forms a pretty design for our blanket, repeatedly hearing examples of God's love for us establishes the message of God's goodness in our thinking.
God commands us to teach the next generation His ways.
"We will not hide them from their children, showing to the generation to come the praises of the LORD, and his strength, and his wonderful works that he hath done."
PSALM 78:4 KJV

BROKEN BUT BETTER

Millie tried not to look in the mirror as she passed by it to turn on the shower, but her broken body had a magnetism about it that drew her attention. After a quick glance at herself, she averted her head from the mastectomy scars slashing their fresh, red streaks across her torso. The tears rolling down her cheeks in the shower felt hotter than the water.

"God, how do I go on from here? I feel so shattered, so broken. How do I live a whole life again in this disfigured body?" Millie felt powerless to overcome her feelings of uselessness.

The day loomed ahead like a blank canvas, only she couldn't find any colors to paint on it. At the thought of color, her friend's invitation to take a quilting class popped into her mind. Quilts radiated color. By the time she had dried and put on her clothes, she'd decided to do it. Maybe in class she'd think about something else besides her disfigurement.

Soon Millie lost herself in the delight of blending colors and pleasing designs from the rows of attractive fabric bolts. "Thanks," she said with a smile when her classmates complimented her choices. The process of cutting out pieces for the Star of the East pattern made her think of the cuts on her body. Here she was taking whole fabric, attractive as it lay all in one piece, and cutting it up into small diamonds, triangles, and squares. They didn't look like much by themselves; certainly not as attractive as the whole length of material had looked. However, when she pinned them together they formed an elegant star. Pieces that looked useless by themselves formed a beautiful design, and together they looked far lovelier than any one of the fabrics alone. She learned to take care as she cut in order for her pieces to fit perfectly. She thanked God for taking care of her as the surgeon had used his skill on her body.

Millie wasted no time putting her finished quilt to use. By day it decorated her bed; and in the evening she and her husband wrapped up in it when they watched TV. Neither did she waste any more time feeling useless. As a volunteer, she began to go to the hospitals and visit other mastectomy patients. She taught them exercises to prevent swelling and restore mobility to their arms, and she brought comfort born from shared pain.

God took the broken pieces of Millie's life and put them together into a new pattern and formed a useful life. Her grateful patients loved her. Millie came to appreciate the suffering of Jesus on the cross. He was broken for the benefit of all mankind.

⁓

GOD'S PATTERN

"And when he had given thanks,
he brake it, and said,
Take, eat: this is my body,
which is broken for you:
this do in remembrance of me."
1 CORINTHIANS 11:24 KJV

On a smaller scale, God takes our brokenness,
as He took Christ's, and forms a beautiful
new pattern for our lives.

FOREVER

*I remember the days of old; I meditate on all thy works;
I muse on the work of thy hands.*
PSALM 143:5 KJV

"It's me, Grandma, Lucy. May I come in?" Lucy peered through the screen door where she could see her grandmother stitching on her latest quilt in the sunroom.

"Come in." Grandma motioned to Lucy with her hand. "What a sight you and baby Kelly make for my old eyes." Grandma reached an arm out to hug Lucy's waist. "Excuse me if I don't get up. I'm hurrying to get this quilt done before your brother Jason's wedding. Put the baby on the floor near my feet so I can watch her while I stitch."

"Why do you make so many quilts, Grandma?" Lucy watched as her grandmother pulled her needle in and out of her California Star quilt.

"I reckon you're too young to understand. I feel like I'm writing a little bit of history when I make a quilt. Some quilts tell stories about events in the history of our nation. Others are silent witnesses to the love of one person for another, like this quilt I'm making for your brother. I like to think I'm making Jason's life more comfortable with every patch I sew. Since a quilt takes so much time, it demonstrates my love."

"Wouldn't it be easier to buy a wedding gift?" Lucy asked.

"Easier, maybe, but it wouldn't represent my good wishes as well as this quilt. If I could stitch perpetual happiness, health, and joy into this comforter, I'd do it. Since I don't have that kind of supernatural power, I satisfy myself with sewing a pretty pattern and praying all the while I stitch for God to supply Jason's life with those blessings."

"I know you love me every morning when I make my bed and pull up the Wedding Ring quilt you made for me." Lucy leaned over and dropped a kiss on Grandma's forehead.

"Maybe my greatest motivation to quilt is striving for a certain amount of immortality. This quilt will still be warming Jason when I'm dead and gone. I hope it'll help him remember me."

"Oops." Lucy wiped Kelly's mouth when she spit up.

"I plan to make little Kelly a quilt next. Then if she never gets to know me as a grown-up, she'll know she once had a great-grandma who loved her because she'll own and handle my quilt."

"I'll always remember you, Grandma, with or without a quilt."

"I'm glad Jesus made a way for us to live forever in heaven and spend eternity with our loved ones who believe in Him, but when I make a quilt I like to think I'm making a memory jogger for the loved ones I leave behind. Maybe even a couple of generations after me will think a few warm thoughts about old Grandma Brown."

God supplied every human with immortality when we were born. Where we spend it depends on whether we accept Jesus as our Savior. The works of God's hand in our lives live on forever without deteriorating and rotting with age as our quilts will. Because of God's work, we have the choice of living forever with God where we will be reunited with our Christian loved ones.

GOD'S PATTERN
God designed our spirits to live forever.
Our search for immortality is fulfilled when
we make Jesus our Lord and Savior.

THE MARVELOUS MIDDLE

Though you have not seen him, you love him;
and even though you do not see him now,
you believe in him and are filled with
an inexpressible and glorious joy.
1 PETER 1:8 NIV

S ettle down," Laura said to her daughter, Candy. Laura twisted around in her chair at the quilt frame to give her a stern look. "Why don't you bring out the new puzzle for the children to put together while their mamas quilt?" She hoped the toy would buy some peace for the friends who had come to her house to quilt together.

The puzzle failed to hold the attention of the younger children, and the women's conversation leap-frogged over a steady stream of requests, complaints, or squabbles.

"Mothers have awesome mental skills to hang onto a thought through unlimited interruptions. Have we completed a sentence this morning without stopping in the middle?" Laura stuck her needle in the blue material in front of her and turned to unfasten Candy's overall straps in order for her to visit the bathroom. She plucked off a piece of Dacron polyfill that had migrated from the middle layer of the quilt to her daughter's rompers.

As lunch neared, the children's dispositions deteriorated.

"They lost a piece to my new puzzle." Candy jogged her mother's elbow, her mouth turned down into a classic pout.

"It has to be around somewhere. Did you look on the floor?"

In spite of the interruptions, the friends continued and

finished stitching a large section of the quilt before they stopped for lunch.

After lunch, the ladies seated themselves for one more short session. Hunter, the smallest boy, cuddled up with a quilt on the floor and fell asleep almost before putting his middle fingers in his mouth.

"Uh-oh." Laura laid down her needle and began to feel around the quilt. "I think I've found the puzzle piece."

Molly reached over and kneaded the quilt with one hand underneath and one on top. "You sure did. I can feel the little nibs on it."

"The trouble is that seven rows of stitches lie between the piece and the open edge. There's no way to get to it without ripping out a big chunk of this morning's work."

"It's a pretty thin piece of cardboard and tiny; could we pretend we never found it?"

Molly chuckled. "You know, like today's popular philosophy—if you don't see it, it doesn't matter."

Laura picked up her ripper and began to remove the little stitches. "It matters to Candy. She can't finish her puzzle without it. You make me think. What's hidden away in the middle of my personality you don't see and don't know about unless you happen to feel the lump it makes?"

Molly sat down beside Laura and began to help take out stitches. "Our spiritual life is like the middle of the quilt; it gives substance to us and warms our hearts but is invisible to the eye. I imagine God doesn't want lumps in the middle of our filling."

"Guess God is a little bit like the middle of a quilt, too. We can't see Him, but we know He's there by the warmth and blessings He wraps around us."

GOD'S PATTERN

Although we don't see God,
we want Him in the middle of
our lives providing for us.
His presence and love give our lives
meaning and allow us to rest like
the baby rested on the quilt on the floor.

EAGER ANTICIPATION

Let us be glad and rejoice,
and give honour to him:
for the marriage of the Lamb is come,
and his wife hath made herself ready.
And to her was granted that she should
be arrayed in fine linen, clean and white:
for the fine linen is the righteousness of saints.
REVELATION 19:7–8 KJV

Bertha finished slicing her Sally Lund bread and laid the platter beside the golden butter. Giving the soup a final stir, she began ladling it into Mother's Wedgwood china bowls while her mother set out a plate of sugar cookies. "It's time for a recess to eat," she called to her extended family bent over the quilting frame.

The women stood and stretched their backs before moving toward the food. Too excited to eat, Bertha examined the morning's work on her wedding quilt. In between wreaths formed of red cherries and green leaves, muslin blocks held outlines of the handprints of her family, four generations. Under every hand, red thread spelled out the person's name and birth date. Bertha's sister had even made a square with her one-year-old daughter's handprint. Bertha stroked the flowers that formed a large heart in the middle of the quilt with her name and Mark's in the center.

"It's almost too beautiful to use."

"You'd better put this quilt on your guest bed and use it only for special occasions. It's too fancy to risk babies spitting up or diapers overflowing on it," Mother warned.

"I'll take good care of it because the best part is having these hand outlines of my family. I love everyone so much." Bertha hugged her aunt who stood nearest to her. "Maybe Pennsylvania won't feel so far away when I look at this quilt on a Kansas homestead." A shadow passed over her face because her new life with Mark meant leaving her family behind.

"Is your wedding dress finished?" Bertha's cousin spoke up to fill in the awkward silence as the family thought about how far away Bertha would live.

"Nearly, but you can't see it until I walk down the aisle of the church." Bertha hugged herself and gave a shiver of anticipation.

"Not even of a swatch of the material?"

"Well, maybe a swatch." Bertha ran into a bedroom to bring out a sample of the airy white lawn fabric.

Making an extra fancy quilt to celebrate a wedding was a custom in the earlier days of our nation. Participation in the construction of the wedding quilt offered a way for family and friends to convey love and support for the bride and give tangible help to outfitting her first home.

Even today, a girl goes to great lengths to become a beautiful bride for her bridegroom. Brides spend quantities of time, energy, and money on their preparations. Whatever sacrifices are involved seem small to the bride who is consumed with love for her bridegroom. In the picture of the marriage of Christ and His church, believers are symbolized as the bride of Christ. It is appropriate for us to lavish time and energy in preparing ourselves to greet our bridegroom with spiritual beauty. No effort is too great to make ourselves ready to please Christ.

GOD'S PATTERN
God supplies us with His righteousness
in order that we may prepare ourselves
to be a suitable bride for Christ.

BEARING UP

*Thy servant slew both the lion and the bear: and this
uncircumcised Philistine shall be as one of them,
seeing he hath defied the armies of the living God.
David said moreover, The LORD that delivered me
out of the paw of the lion, and out of the paw of the bear,
he will deliver me out of the hand of this Philistine.
And Saul said unto David, Go, and the LORD be with thee.*
1 SAMUEL 17:36–37 KJV

I t doesn't fit together right." Deanne threw the red and white
squares onto Rene's lap. "I thought you said this is an easy
quilt for a beginner."

"The Bear Paw pattern usually works well. It's all straight
lines with no curves to throw things out of kilter." Rene studied
the pieces.

"'You can't go wrong' is what you said. Well, something's
wrong. It looks weird when I sew the squares together." She
stabbed the offending design with her finger. "The points
of the toes are going every which way, and some are lots
smaller than others." A giggle snuck up and overpowered her
frustration. "The bear must have been a cripple."

"Did you check each block with a 'square up' ruler to be
sure every one made a perfect square before you started the
next piece?"

"Check each block? The directions only said eight rows
of ten blocks, so I made eighty blocks full speed ahead, but
nothing works together. The edges are uneven along the sides

when I try to sew this monstrosity into a complete quilt top."

Tugging at the material, Rene laid the pieces on a table. "I'm not sure what to do."

"I know exactly what to do with this quilt." Deanne picked up a nearby wastebasket and, holding it at the edge of the table, pushed the quilt pieces into it with an emphatic swipe of her arm. She slammed her sewing machine back into its case and marched into the kitchen. In a moment she returned and slapped a cookbook in front of Rene, who sat in her chair, trying to keep her mouth from gaping open.

"Here's something I understand. I follow the cookbook recipe instructions, and I have a lovely, light cake or creamy pudding for my efforts. I'll leave the quilting to you and feed you while you do it."

Although Deanne refused to try the Bear Paw pattern again, she did stick with learning to quilt in spite of her early frustrations. As she grew in knowledge of what the craft required, she developed more patience and came to appreciate God's faithfulness to her in spite of the imperfections of her character. Many times when she'd catch herself not fitting into God's plan, she'd think of the Bear Paw quilt and adopt a more cooperative attitude.

~

GOD'S PATTERN

The purpose of His design for us is to form a
beautiful design for the kingdom of God.
Frustration grates our soul, but we can
allow God to use it to refine our character.
Fitting into His pattern brings us the skill of
discerning good in life's lows as well as the highs.

WATCH OUT

We are confident, I say,
and willing rather to be absent from the body,
and to be present with the Lord.
2 CORINTHIANS 5:8 KJV

Grandmother Konane reached a hand out from under the sheet and touched her granddaughter. "The family quilts. . ." Her waning strength reduced her voice to a whisper. "Guard them from prying eyes. Treasure them. They record the love, feelings, and events of our ancestors. Check every week for mildew and be vigilant against the pests that have destroyed so many Hawaiian quilts."

She struggled to raise her shoulders from the bed. "Look in the cedar chest for my Royal Flag quilt. Take out the one where all the red and blue strips run up and down. I made it, and my *mana* rests in that quilt. . . ." Too weak to continue, her voice trailed off.

"Rest, Grandmother. I'll find it and bring it to your bedroom, and you can tell me if I've located the quilt your spirit rests in." Lani squeezed her grandmother's hand before walking through the door to an anteroom.

When the maid waiting for instructions saw how the tears blurred Lani's vision, she helped lift the quilts from the chest. Lani stood by the light from the window and read the date Grandmother had embroidered on the back of the two-color Royal Hawaiian Flag quilt.

"When Grandmother made this in 1879, she was fifty years old," Lani told the maid who helped her unfold the quilt. Lani looked out over the clear blue Malala Bay from her Honolulu home. "What a lot of Hawaiian history she has seen. She refused to make a Hawaiian Flag quilt after the annexation to the United States in 1898. I didn't know she had made so many quilts. I guess it's because we Hawaiians carefully guard our quilt patterns so no one will copy them. I seldom saw Grandmother's Hawaiian quilts displayed."

Carrying the quilt, Lani returned to her grandmother's bedside and found her asleep. Pulling up a chair, she waited to see if she had found the right comforter. Since it felt hot on her lap, she laid it on a nearby table. In Hawaii, quilts were for artistic expression, not warmth.

Grandmother smiled when she opened her eyes and saw Lani with the quilt. "My spirit rests here," she said, pointing to the red and blue flag. "Burn it when I die."

The strength of her grip surprised Lani. "I don't want you to die."

"Hush, child, I know my days are few. Burn the quilt when my last breath leaves."

"But it's so beautiful, and we want something to remember you by."

"I've made other quilts and lots of Royal Hawaiian Flag quilts. This one you are to burn to protect my *mana*. Will you carry out my wishes, or must I ask another?"

"Yes, Grandmother." Now Lani's voice sounded weaker than her grandmother's.

How grateful we are that our spirit doesn't linger around the earth after we die, haunting places or things. Instead, those of us who have received Jesus into our lives will live in the presence of God for all eternity.

Because Hawaiians carefully guarded their quilt patterns, not wanting anyone to copy them, Hawaiian quilts were not often displayed. Today's quilter is eager to share patterns and expertise with others.

GOD'S PATTERN
Our spirit lives forever.
God made a plan that provides for our spirit
to live eternally with God.
God wants us to share the pattern
He designed for eternal life with others.

PATIENCE

For ye have need of patience,
that, after ye have done the will of God,
ye might receive the promise.
HEBREWS 10:36 KJV

And let us not be weary in well doing:
for in due season we shall reap,
if we faint not.
GALATIANS 6:9 KJV

What's this?" Ben opened the next box on the attic shelf.

"A quilt I started," Clara answered. "I never finished because it was taking so long."

"You're a fine one to talk. You're always fussing with me because I didn't finish something. You never did get off my back about the unfinished bird feeder."

"I'd forgotten how pretty the fan pattern is." Clara ignored her son, pulled the half-finished coverlet out of the box, and held it up to the faint attic light.

"Mother, you're always saying, 'Finish what you start.'" Ben enjoyed feeling like he had the upper hand and continued to tease his mother.

"Maybe I *will* finish this. I like how I shaded the blues from light to dark. Let's take it down and look at it in good light. I think I stopped when I started doing the PTA treasurer's job.

"Remember my friend Marge? She and I made quilts together. She paid someone to quilt hers after she finished piecing the top. I never finished the top. Some people like the piecing best and some people like the quilting part."

"The man who owns the department store where I work likes to piece quilts on a machine." Ben carried the quilt down the attic ladder. "He has no patience for quilting and always hires it out."

Quilting by machine has changed the time required to make a quilt. By hand, the process takes time. Any task or hobby that requires a long time from start to finish is profitable for character development. When a person learns to delay gratification for a better reward in the end, he or she develops patience. Patience helps us when we find ourselves in situations that are beyond our control.

Sometimes we are not able to find answers for our circumstances in a hurry. Certainly in rearing children, we can't hasten their maturing. As children grow, they try our patience. Qualities important to adult living don't spring into existence overnight. When we find ourselves powerless in the face of adversities, we will press through to reap the fruit of our efforts if we have learned not to faint at difficulties. First comes the patience and then the promise.

GOD'S PATTERN
God's promises are steadfast.
He gives the strength to hold on to them
even when we feel weary and faint.

BLEEDING

But one of the soldiers with a spear pierced his side,
and forthwith came there out blood and water.
JOHN 19:34 KJV

O uch." The thin, sharp needle penetrated Cher's finger so deeply it left a scarlet trail as she pulled her hand out from underneath the quilt. Before she realized how much she was bleeding, bright drops splattered on her pineapple appliquéd square.

Recovery from the jab did not concern Cher nearly as much as the stains on her quilt. "Can you get these stains out, Mr. Barr?" Cher asked the dry cleaner where she took her quilt, hoping for help.

"That depends. It looks like you've already worked on them. What did you try?"

"First I used cold water. When those stubborn places on the pineapple shapes didn't come out," Cher pointed to the serrated points of the golden fabric, "I tried a commercial stain remover. Next, I tried hair spray. My neighbor said that always works, but it didn't."

The man behind the counter sighed as he shook his head. "No, it often sets a stain. Did you ever let hot water touch it?"

"Well, maybe a little when I washed out the hair spray." A sinking feeling dropped into Cher's middle when she saw Mr. Barr frown and stroke the remaining lock of hair he plastered across the top of his head.

"If you've put hot water on blood stains, we probably can't remove them completely."

"I've spent hours and days, no, weeks on this quilt," Cher wailed. "It's a gift for my sister's twenty-fifth wedding anniversary." She struggled to bring her voice back to a normal level. "Do something."

"We can try bleach on the white background, but bleach will affect the printed fabric. It often fades colors." Mr. Barr tugged his hair until it fell to the side, leaving his shiny head bare.

Afraid Mr. Barr was right and her quilt would never again look as good as new, Cher did not wait to see the result. She stopped at the store on the way home and bought supplies to begin another quilt right away.

The clerk was adamant that she should use a size nine needle when doing the appliqué and switch to a size ten needle when she began quilting. She winced when she laid out her needles, realizing what had caused her to ruin her project. Not owning the right sizes, she had substituted a size seven needle. In her struggle to push the too large needle through all the layers, she had resorted to force and stabbed herself hard.

Fretting over her deadline, she changed the design of her pineapples, giving them smooth sides instead of serrated and reduced their number in order to minimize the time required to cut and stitch a new top. "Sis is worth my best; I'll do whatever it takes to get a pretty quilt to her by her anniversary."

When Jesus shed His blood on the cross, He didn't take shortcuts but gave His best—to give us the gift of eternal life. We could not earn it even if we smoothed the sides of our lives and stitched the pieces with all our might. The blood and water which flowed when the Roman soldier pierced His side brought horror and grief to the bystanders, but it brought a witness to His followers throughout the centuries that Jesus had secured life for them at the sacrifice of His blood.

GOD'S PATTERN

His blood shed on the cross
made complete atonement for our sin.
By accepting His sacrifice,
we attain salvation.
The stains of our life are removed.

YOU'RE SOMEBODY

To the praise of the glory of his grace,
wherein he hath made us accepted in the beloved.
EPHESIANS 1:6 KJV

"I'm sorry I came here. My room is too small, and I'm lonely. I don't know anybody who lives here," Gladys complained to her visitor, Roma, about the nursing home where she had lived for only two weeks.

"Next time I come, I'll bring you lots of company. Wouldn't it be fun to see the Sunday school class you used to teach?" Since Roma had taken over the class, she faithfully stayed in touch with Gladys, the retired church secretary.

"Can't have them in this tiny place." Gladys waved her arm, indicating her room. "Anyway, they've grown up a lot since I taught them. They won't want to bother with an old lady like me."

The next day, during Roma's ninth-grade Sunday school class, she told the girls how hard it is for some older people to adjust to new surroundings. The girls jumped at Roma's idea of making and taking a lap quilt to Gladys.

Each girl embroidered her name on a square of material she brought from home. Roma embroidered "With love from your Sunday school class" on the center square and sewed the squares together. The girls had a quilt-tying party at Roma's house and planned a celebration to present the gift.

Ten girls arrived early at the nursing home to decorate the lounge with crepe paper and banners, broadcasting their love for Gladys. They set out punch and cookies. Meanwhile, the staff brought many of the other residents into the lounge. Then Roma went to Gladys's room, fluffed her gray hair into a pretty frame around her face, settled her into a wheelchair, and rolled her into the lounge.

"Surprise!" the girls shouted. For a moment, Roma wondered if she'd used bad judgment, surprising an eighty-six-year-old woman; but, after a stunned look, a wide smile stretched Gladys's thin lips and pumped bright color into her cheeks.

"We made you a present." The tallest girl put the puffy package on Gladys' lap. Gladys's smile competed with tears when she saw what the girls had made for her. As the other residents crowded around to admire the lap quilt, the smile won.

The girls arranged themselves on the steps in the lobby and sang hymns and choruses, urged on by the applause and appreciation of their audience. Soon old, wavering voices joined young vibrant ones to lift praises to God.

While the residents enjoyed the refreshments, Gladys kept stroking the quilt and saying, "I can't believe you did this."

When she mailed a thank-you note to the class, the nursing home staff enclosed a note.

You girls did not realize you were giving your former Sunday school teacher a gift more important than the lap quilt which warms her body as she sits in her wheelchair. The attention you gave increased her importance in the eyes of the other residents and helped her feel accepted in our little community.

God understands our need for acceptance and will provide it at the right time. Times of loneliness or times of experiencing rejection may also bring about the design of God for our lives.

We can allow our need for acceptance to drive us closer to God and deepen our understanding of His favor.

GOD'S PATTERN

When the rejection or neglect of people grieves us,
we can cover ourselves with the acceptance of
God and grow warm in His presence.
Human companionship is attracted to us as our
demeanor grows cheerful from delighting in Him.

GOD'S STITCHERY

I will praise thee;
for I am fearfully and wonderfully made:
marvellous are thy works.
PSALM 139:14 KJV

"What's this?" Joanne pointed to the blue lines that meandered around Polly's quilt.

"They're washable marks to guide my quilting stitches." Polly showed Joanne a section where she had already stitched the lines with white thread on the white muslin.

"But it doesn't have any design or consistent pattern. It just wanders around. Sorta reminds me of the lines my kindergartner scribbles all over her paper before she fills them in with her crayons."

"Maybe it's a notch above a kindergarten scribble." Polly decided not to take offense. "You'll notice none of the lines cross over each other. It's called Stepple quilting. I know it seems aimless, but it really holds the layers of material together well, and it serves the purpose of keeping the fabric flat."

"I have to admit the places you have already finished look nice once you got rid of the blue line. Is the line hard to take out? It looks like ink."

"It disappears the minute I put cold water on it. Hot water is a no-no. It sets the color instead of making it vanish."

Sometimes we feel as if the pattern of our lives has become aimless and without color. We don't understand the design that our circumstances are drawing. We may feel we have lost our purpose. We endure these stages better if we remember God is the Master quilter of our lives. He began with a marvelous plan, and He knows the finest way to achieve it. He knows the right places to establish a flatness and lack of color to provide a pleasing contrast to the patterns where He stitches vivid events and triumphs into our lives. The blue marker, which disappears when touched by cold water, reminds us that the ugly marks sin writes on our souls disappear with the touch of God's forgiveness. When we repent from bad choices and attitudes, God is faithful to cleanse us from the stain of sin.

GOD'S PATTERN

When God formed us,
He knew His wonderful plan for our lives.
Even when we have messed up His plan,
He continues to work His design in us
and provide the stitches to hold us together.

THE SCARLET QUILT

And be ye kind one to another,
tenderhearted, forgiving one another,
even as God for Christ's sake hath forgiven you.
EPHESIANS 4:32 KJV

Trish, have you met Mona?" Sandy reached out to stop her friend Trish, who was passing down the church aisle after the service. "Mona's been coming to our church for about a month now."

Trish gave the young girl a sideways hug. Mona's advanced pregnancy made any other kind impossible. "When's the baby due?"

"December second."

Mona looked at the floor, and Trish gave Sandy a questioning look.

"Maybe one of your teenagers could help Mona after school when the baby is born," Sandy suggested.

"Sure, do you have other children?" Trish asked.

"No."

Trish felt Sandy's knuckles jab her in the back, and Trish decided she'd better stop with the questions. "What's going on?" she asked when Mona had moved down the aisle. "What's with the kidney punch?"

"The daddy of Mona's baby disappeared when he learned she was pregnant. They never married. I guess after that the Lord reminded Mona of her childhood roots in the church."

"She's brave to come back. I hope people will hold their

tongues and show kindness."

Indeed, the church ladies outdid themselves showing kindness. Although the news of Mona's situation traveled fast, the ladies' responses reflected the character of Jesus. Instead of asking embarrassing questions about where Daddy was, the congregation asked what she needed. The women decided that the innocent child, conceived in lust, would receive love and welcome in God's church family.

Trish took a special interest in the situation. "Do you notice how embarrassed Mona seems?" Trish asked Sandy. "She has a hard time lifting her eyes to meet anyone's gaze when we talk to her. How can we make her feel accepted? We may not have had our babies out of wedlock, but we've all made mistakes we regret and needed God's forgiveness."

The women's prayer circle decided to host a baby shower and to make a quilt for the event. Using baby colors, each woman pieced a block about the love of God. In order to finish the blanket before the shower, they tied it together with yarn instead of quilting it.

The attendance of dozens of women pleased the hostesses and overwhelmed Mona. With each gift she unwrapped, her eyes grew larger. As the stack of gifts grew, Trish said, "We're determined to make your li'l punkin the best outfitted kid in the church."

With her eyes studying her shoes, Mona stammered her thanks. Everyone fell silent to watch her open the last gift, the quilt. "Do you really love me this much?" Mona whispered as she lifted the quilt from its tissue paper cocoon. When Mona stood to show everyone the quilt, she lifted her head and looked around the room. "How can you love me enough to do all this when I'm. . .I'm. . .I've made a lot of mistakes?" Her chin quivered.

"Hey, we all needed the death of Jesus on the cross to

cover our mistakes." Sandy took Mona's hand. "Since God's forgiveness means He's forgotten the mistake, we chose not to dwell on it also."

"How many people fit into the hospital waiting room?" Trish asked. "We all want to come dance with the angels when the baby is born."

"Hear that, li'l punkin? You have a welcome committee waiting." Mona lifted her head and looked from face to face. She didn't know the broad smiles were as much for her ability to look them in the eye as for her words.

The women's tender kindness gave Mona a glimpse of God's grace, which helped her accept His forgiveness. After the gift of the quilt, she held her head up and faced the challenges of her life, confident that God did not reject her because of her sin but, rather, had provided a way to erase it.

GOD'S PATTERN

When we offer kindness and forgiveness
for others in times of failure,
we demonstrate God's mercy.
We all require the depths of His grace
for our daily living.

DOG BEGONE

And he said, Draw not nigh hither:
put off thy shoes from off thy feet,
for the place whereon thou standest is holy ground.
EXODUS 3:5 KJV

"Good-bye." Shannon stood in the doorway and waved as her quilt guild walked down the driveway to their cars. "I'll attach the entry information to each quilt before I bring them to the hotel for the exhibit."

Her three hounds bounded into the house while she held the door open.

"Don't let those dogs in the house while you have our quilts spread out over your floor." Winona slammed her car door and marched back up the walk and into the front door. "Dogs are as bad as moths for quilts. I can't believe you let those dogs in, Shannon." She took Shannon's arm and pulled her toward the family room where the women had left their quilts spread out over the floor. "If I'd known you had dogs, three no less, I'd have never left my quilt here."

She paused at the doorway, her mouth dropping open. There the three hounds were stepping carefully between the quilts, picking the narrow inches in between the comforters to put their feet. Not a single paw step fell on the quilts.

When Bongo, the largest hound, reached the recliner, he jumped up and began to curl around and around until he was satisfied with his position and dropped down with a sigh. The other two hounds eased their way toward the sofa on the far wall. Winona held her breath while Bingo sidled past her quilt. He leaped heavily onto a pillow and looked back at Winona with mournful eyes that seemed aggrieved at her distrust of him.

"Well, I never. . ." Winona stopped, unable to hide her surprise. "Every dog I know makes a beeline for a quilt as if the whole purpose of making one is to furnish the pooch with a soft nap."

Shannon laughed and took Winona's hand off her arm where it was leaving a mark from her tense grip. "Not my bassets. You saw them take great pains not to step on them. Avoiding ten big quilts to get to the couch took some doing."

"Maybe they're careful because we're looking. I'll bet if we went into the living room and sneaked back in a few minutes, they'd all have picked out the softest ones for a nap."

"I don't know why, but they seem to know the quilts are off-limits for them. Wish they felt the same way about the furniture." Shannon gave a wry smile.

For some mysterious reason, Shannon's dogs respected the work of the quilters. Good manners taught at a young age help us learn to show consideration to others and their property. Respecting others even when they annoy us comes easier when we recognize everyone is the creation of God. When we defer to others, we take care not to step on their feelings or hurt them.

Honoring God leads us to live carefully around the world of His creation, our earth. A little extra thought helps us preserve the things of nature He created for us to enjoy. Most important, we hold God in the highest esteem, for He alone is holy. He is worthy of our awe and reverence.

GOD'S PATTERN

As the people in biblical days removed their shoes to demonstrate their reverence, our adoration of God causes us to desire to remove any steps that would not honor our God.

The Quarrel

And into an inheritance that can never perish, spoil or fade—
kept in heaven for you.
1 PETER 1:4 NIV

"I suppose you want Mother's wedding album, too." Gina didn't try to hide the sarcasm in her voice as she pulled the book off the shelf and held it over a packing box.

"I am the oldest; and since I host all the family gatherings, it makes sense for me to keep it where people will have the most opportunity to see it." Cora reached for the leather volume.

Gina bit her tongue against the sharp words pounding across her mind. Beginning the day their mother died, the sisters had argued over the distribution of her possessions.

By the time the daughters began to clean out the attic, hostility prickled as badly as the heat in the air. When Gina opened a black plastic garbage bag, she swallowed a gasp of delight. It was full of lovely fabric scraps. *Perfect for my quilting,* she thought and tucked it over in a corner, planning to carry it down the steps and out to her car unnoticed later.

However, her plan crumbled when she came across two more garbage bags of scraps. *Three bags of scraps are too many to sneak out of the attic,* she thought. She turned when she heard Cora chortle behind her.

There her sister was, leaning over two more garbage bags piled to the top with leftover pieces of material from some of their mother's many projects. "Perfect. I can make my kids quilts from these."

"You'll never do it. You just talk about quilting," Gina protested. "I'll really use them. I should get the bags."

"Look, you're standing by two bags and there's another one over in the corner." Cora gestured toward the bag Gina had thought she'd hidden. "We'll split them."

"I quilt twice as much as you." Gina didn't try to keep her voice down.

"Now that all the kids are in school, I'm going to do more."

"Where are you?" At the call of their husbands arriving to take them to dinner, the sisters stopped arguing and clambered down to wash up.

The next morning when the sisters climbed to the attic, Cora's voice shrilled with rage. "Where are the fabric scraps?"

Gina didn't answer.

"Did you take them? You did. I can tell by your face. You took them all. You didn't even leave me one."

Gina backed down the stairs at the sight of her sister's face.

Angry words and unleashed hostility rang through the house, ending with both sisters screeching out of the driveway in their cars. The girls haven't spoken to each other since. A relationship of a lifetime cut to shreds because of five garbage bags of scraps. The inheritance of the sisters drove a wedge and spoiled their peace.

Parents who don't want their children quarreling over their possessions after they die are wise to write wills to eliminate arguing. Better yet, parents should try to raise their children to value relationships over possessions. Our wise heavenly Father has prepared a better inheritance for us than any human parent can provide. It doesn't fade like fabric scraps will surely do. It lasts forever, and its value is beyond measure.

❧

GOD'S PATTERN

God's will is for us to inherit eternal life and understand that which comes later is better than that which comes first. This life pales in comparison to life everlasting.

DID YOU KNOW?

Yea, the darkness hideth not from thee;
but the night shineth as the day:
the darkness and the light are both alike to thee.
PSALM 139:12 KJV

The Woods family always referred to the summer of Kenny's illness as the dark summer. While the frequently cloudy days cast gloom over the landscape of their home, the gray atmosphere that shrouded the inside of the Woodses' home, challenged even the electric lights to dispel it. Three-year-old Kenny suffered from a dangerous disease.

Billy and his brother Brian never let on to their friends, but they welcomed the rainy days when they worked on their quilts while their mother stitched hers. Right after school closed in June, Mother had helped them cut the diamond and square shapes for their Tumbling Block pattern. When the boys arranged the pieces correctly, contrasting the light squares with the dark diamonds, the shapes looked like real, three-dimensional blocks.

As the summer passed, the boys took turns sharing jokes with their little brother, who lay in a bed while they worked on their quilts. Kenny enjoyed the companionship, and his big brothers liked the sense of accomplishment they gained from watching their Tumbling Block project grow. The reward of watching Kenny enjoy the blocks on their quilt when he was too sick to play with real blocks kept them diligently returning to their stitching all summer long. Mom said that someday the treatments would make Kenny strong enough to build a block tower with real blocks. In the meantime he liked to trace his finger around the block outlines and try to figure out how flat material could look like real cubes.

Whenever a friend rang the doorbell, Billy and Brian stuffed their quilts under a chair before running to answer it. One day their next door neighbor didn't do the courtesy of ringing the bell. Tom marched unannounced into the house to find the boys with their quilts in their laps. Billy and Brian froze, their needles in their hands. Mrs. Woods interrupted Tom's derisive whoop before he could follow it up with scornful words.

"Tom, if you behave yourself, you can join the boys. They're training to be president of the United States."

All three boys stared at Mrs. Woods in disbelief.

"When Dwight D. Eisenhower and Calvin Coolidge were boys, probably around the same age as you fellows, they helped their mothers make quilts. Dwight Eisenhower made a Tumbling Block quilt just like the ones Billy and Brian are working on, and Calvin Coolidge made a Baby Block quilt, which is the same pattern only using pastel colors suitable for babies."

"What's that got to do with being president?" Tom managed to stop gaping and ask.

"They learned not to succumb to peer pressure by doing something considered unusual for boys. They learned to examine their actions for value instead of making their decisions for appearances. By learning to stand alone they became men who were willing to stick by their principles when they were grown. A very important quality for a president, don't you think?"

"Yes, ma'am." Tom stood, feeling awkward.

"Tell you what. You can help entertain Kenny by telling him about your day. A little distraction brightens his outlook after his treatments."

"Kinda like our bright quilts," Billy said. "The contrast

of the dark material lying next to the light material makes the cubes look so real."

"The boys and I will put everything away while you talk. We were nearly ready to stop for pizza. Would you like to have lunch with us?"

"Yes, ma'am." This time Tom's voice sounded pleased.

Learning new skills stretches our abilities and expands our horizons. A willingness to risk the label of being different opens us up to explore new talents and more profitable attitudes. In the New Testament, Peter broke from the accepted path when he took the good news of the gospel to the Gentiles. Millions of Christians are thankful he found the courage to break traditions and preach to non-Jewish people.

GOD'S PATTERN
Remain flexible and listen for God's direction.
"For thou wilt light my candle:
the LORD my God will enlighten my darkness."
PSALM 18:28 KJV

HAPPY FACES

*Happy is he that hath the God of Jacob for his help,
whose hope is in the LORD his God.*
PSALM 146:5 KJV

Sally bit her lip as she concentrated on her crayon picture. Seated next to her, Mary Jo chewed on a corner of her Brownie uniform handkerchief. Unusual quiet reigned as the entire Brownie troop plied their fabric crayons to their muslin squares.

"I'll draw a rainbow if you'll make a flower under it," Sally told Mary Jo. "Fern likes rainbows."

"I'm drawing a sun with my flowers," another Brownie Scout piped up.

"I'm making lots of hearts so Fern will know we love her. When can Fern come back to our Brownie meeting?" Mary Jo asked.

"Probably not for several months. Both she and her brother have a lot of injuries from the accident. Getting well will take time," the troop leader said.

"I'm ready to start on her brother's quilt. What can we draw for Grady's quilt?" Mary Jo asked.

"Boys don't want lots of hearts and flowers." Sally shared her wisdom learned from a large family of brothers. "They like smiley faces, especially if they feel sick."

"Will Grady throw up on our quilt?" Mary Jo looked up with alarm in her eyes.

"He just broke bones," Sally said. "He didn't break his stomach."

After the girls had drawn their pictures, the troop leader took the squares home and sewed them together. The next week at the Brownie meeting, the girls tied the layers together with bright colored yarn. The mothers drove the troop to the hospital the next day to present their gifts.

The girls found Grady sound asleep from his pain medication. When Sally and Mary Jo spread the cover over his quiet form, tears slid down his mother's cheeks. The deep creases on the single woman's face betrayed the strain she felt from caring for two injured children.

Next everyone visited Fern. Her wide-awake eyes sparkled with delight over the quilt, and her mother, Mrs. Trevor, helped the troop leader hang it on the wall at the end of the bed where she could see it.

"I've felt so alone." Mrs. Trevor reached out her arms and hugged as many girls as she could gather in. "I'll always think of brown as the color of hope because you sweet Brownies came with these gifts of love. Your love has renewed my hope in God."

Our hope for solutions to illness, finances, relationship difficulties, or any type of trouble rests in God. The same faithfulness God showed Jacob in long-ago Bible days is available to us today, and we do count ourselves happy because He stands ready to help us.

GOD'S PATTERN
The God of today continues the pattern
of the faithful God of the Old Testament.
He offers hope for every situation.

MAKE NEW FRIENDS

A man that hath friends must show himself friendly:
and there is a friend that sticketh closer than a brother.
PROVERBS 18:24 KJV

Two are better than one; because they have a
good reward for their labour.
ECCLESIASTES 4:9 KJV

She sat alone on the Florida beach and watched the waves roll toward her bare feet. Children romped far to the right, and the couple on her left slept on a towel.

"This is ridiculous," Megan informed a sand fiddler who scurried past her toes. "I like the beach. I love the cozy feeling of this town. I'm crazy about my new house. And I don't miss the cad I left behind in Mississippi. But I'm so lonely I could cry." And she did, allowing quiet sobs to escape while she sat with her knees drawn up to her chin in case someone passed by and she needed to hide her face.

"That does it. Time to take some steps when I bawl on the beach—my best therapy location." Her eyes traveled unseeing over the newspaper she had brought with her until an ad caught her attention. "That's the answer," Megan said and stuffed her towel, sunscreen, and newspaper into her beach bag. Picking up her chair, she trudged over the sand toward the car. Her trudge became a run when she left the moist sand near the water and the hot ground scorched her feet.

Back home, she dialed the number in the paper while her chicken TV dinner heated in the microwave.

Long after the bell announced her dinner was ready, she was still enjoying an animated conversation with the president of the local quilt guild. "I'll be there, seven o'clock tomorrow night at the library. See you then."

Megan was surprised how quickly she felt comfortable with the guild ladies. Bringing her quilt paved the way for easy conversation. Sharing a hobby in common with the women made her feel friendly and comfortable. Noticing one of the women didn't wear a wedding ring, she shifted her chair nearby, thinking if the woman was also single she might have a free evening. To Megan's delight the lady accepted her invitation for dinner the following week.

In the weeks and months that followed, the quilt guild became the focus of Megan's social life. Her involvement branched out to include other activities with the ladies.

"I don't know what I would have done when I moved here if it wasn't for this guild," she reported one night. "When my husband left me to marry another woman, I thought I had lost forever the advantages of the Bible verse which says two are better than one. But you all make me forget I'm one. I'm no longer lonely."

One of the blessings that accompanies a hobby is the way it opens opportunities for friendships with people one might never have known otherwise. When we are pursuing an area of mutual interest, it helps us overcome shyness. Showing ourselves friendly becomes easier.

GOD'S PATTERN

Friends provide strength to one another.
Shared companionship brightens life.
God's pattern is to look for ways to
include people in our activities
and to avoid being exclusive.

GOD'S PATTERN

Direct my footsteps according to your word;
let no sin rule over me.
PSALM 119:133 NIV

Linda's face twisted with pain when she wrapped in tissue paper the baby blanket her grandmother had knit. "Why, Lord?" Linda laid the blanket on top of the crib sheets in the cardboard carton. The pink and blue yarn showed through the thin paper. Not knowing the sex of the baby, Grandma had used both colors for her gift.

"It could have been all blue, Grandma," Linda whispered. "James was a boy." She stopped to wipe her eyes, almost surprised they could produce any more tears. She had done little else but cry since the miscarriage a month ago. Unable to bear any more regrets, she fled the nursery and ran down the stairs. Without thinking, she punched the phone's automatic dial button for her mother.

"I can't do it." Linda's words were garbled by her sobs. "Everyone says I need to pack all the baby stuff away and get on with living. I tried, but I can't stand it."

In record time Linda's mother wheeled her car into the driveway and let the screen door bang behind her as she entered the house.

"You don't need to do this all by yourself. I'll help you." With their arms wrapped around one another's waists, they climbed up the stairs and entered the silent nursery.

"Do I need to paint over the rocking horse paper border

Joel and I hung? Is that part of putting it all behind me?"

"Of course not. You'll have another baby some day, but you don't want dusty clothes so we'll store these things in the attic in the meantime."

"How do I know I'll ever have another baby? Nothing makes any sense." Linda sank into the rocking chair. She leaned forward to pull the brown teddy bear from behind her back and threw it across the room. "My life is out of control. There's no reason for anything."

"Life feels like that sometimes," Mom said. "I have an idea of what will help. There's a new quilting class starting at the fabric shop in the mall. Nothing like making a quilt to give you a sense of purpose and control."

Desperate for distraction, Linda took the class. She concentrated on cutting the sizes accurately. Planning for the progression of colors from light to dark in her Log Cabin quilt seemed to restore her sense of order. To ensure an attractive overall appearance, she had to design and plan ahead. As she decided which colors to use for her short and long strips, she thought about God, who knew ahead when dark patches would cloud her world. If she could use her dark strips to the best advantage in a small thing like a quilt, she knew God would use the dark places in her life to make a pleasing pattern even if she couldn't see it or understand it yet.

Linda began to trust Him as the Perfect Designer even if she never did understand the "whys" of her experience. "When life feels out of control to me, God is still there," she reassured herself. As she sewed, she found she could pray again. "Order my steps, Lord. Don't let my heartache overpower my love for You."

Each added strip built a pretty blend of colors that created an overall pattern beyond the individual design of each block. Linda was delighted with the results. As her satisfaction grew, she found her joy returning. While she began to enjoy the process of quilting, she began to delight once again in her God and trust Him with her hopes and disappointments.

GOD'S PATTERN

If we keep our heart focused on
the goodness of God,
the Master planner,
we can find hope and encouragement
to weather our storms.

DESIGN FOR WHOLENESS

We who are strong ought to bear
with the failings of the weak
and not to please ourselves.
ROMANS 15:1 NIV

S hasta lay speechless on her hospital bed. All she could do
was look in gratitude at her friends gathered at her bedside.
The group could not have thought of a better gift for her.
Shasta spread the quilt top out on the sheet.

"It's perfect," Shasta stammered, and then the words began
to tumble. "This will be better therapy for me than the chemo
the doctor insists I must take."

"We've basted the twelve blocks to the batting and backing
so it's all ready for you to quilt. We hope the project will fill
time for you while you wait on your treatments and twiddle
your thumbs in doctors' offices," Diane said.

"And here I was worrying about wasting time and feeling
bored for these long weeks ahead. You've given me a great way
to distract myself from my illness and stop worrying about my
health. Tell me who made which block?" she asked and then
answered herself. "I see you each signed them."

Shasta listened with delight as the women chattered about
the squares, telling why they had selected the various patterns
and how the colors all seemed to fit together.

"This package holds the rest of the present." A portable
quilting hoop, a package of needles, a thimble, and a spool of

thread tumbled out of Carrie's sack onto the bed.

"Don't forget this." Diane held up a large, hand-quilted tote bag. "You can use it to carry everything back and forth to the hospital for chemotherapy."

"Our quilt will become my greatest treasure. Line up for hugs." She let go of Carrie to ask, "How did all twelve of you get in here? Isn't it against the rules?"

"We bribed the head nurse. She quilts and said our gift was better than medicine. It didn't hurt to leave her a package of needles. Just don't let her use them on you."

"Bet those thin quilting needles would feel better than the ones she uses." Shasta rolled her eyes.

Shasta faithfully carried her quilting project to her daily treatments. To her surprise, she never tired too much to quilt a little, helping to pass the time faster. Even at home, she quilted although she often fell asleep over her work. Every time worry began to overpower her faith, she picked up the quilt her friends had prepared for her. If her friends' love and concern prompted them to give her a pleasant occupation while she battled for her health, she knew her heavenly Father was preparing and caring for her in an even better manner. The perfect gift not only supplied her need to feel usefully occupied during the long weeks of chemo, but viewing the handiwork of her friends buoyed up her emotional state. When her body was too weak to stitch, she sometimes sat and held the quilt as a tangible way to soak up her friends' love. Embracing the quilt reminded her of her friends and encouraged her to lean upon the strength of her best friend, Jesus.

Shasta used the summer after finishing her chemotherapy to complete the quilt. In addition to the pleasure the work gave her, she believes the project helped her face her illness with an attitude of faith.

God's Word urges us to help the weak. If we ask Him, He will show us creative ways to meet the needs of people when illness, finances, or heartbreak weaken them.

GOD'S PATTERN

The encouragement of others
not only meets tangible needs,
but it undergirds our attitudes,
helping us sustain healthy thoughts
when life seems to crumble around us.
God did not design us to
stand alone in times of trial.

DON'T FORGET ME

*For though I be absent in the flesh, yet am I with you in the spirit,
joying and beholding your order,
and the stedfastness of your faith in Christ.*
COLOSSIANS 2:5 KJV

"You're making another baby quilt? Who's pregnant in our church?" Angie, Melissa's neighbor, held the day's mail for both of them. She plopped into a chair.

"No one. This is for my niece's baby due in March." Melissa continued to appliqué the yellow duck on the pale green background.

"Why go to all that trouble? You'll never see her. She's never come to see you in Nevada, and she's not in Florida for you to see when you go home to visit."

"That's exactly the reason. Welcoming all the family babies connects me with family members I don't have a chance to see."

"They probably don't appreciate the trouble a quilt takes."

"Maybe not, but if I invest myself in my extended family, they'll grow to care about me. I think letters and acts of love enrich my life and theirs." Melissa bit off her thread and positioned a lamb next to the duck. "These family babies are going to grow up and become teenagers faced with all the difficult pressures teens experience today. Maybe knowing they have an aunt in Nevada who cares enough to make a quilt and send them cards will help them make good choices. Pressure to live up to high family expectations never hurts a kid and can help a lot."

"One little quilt does all that! I don't think so." Angie

leaned over to tap Melissa's knee with an envelope. "You're expecting too much mileage from your gift, even if it does represent a lot of work."

"Well, I always pray for the person when I make a quilt and when I send birthday and Christmas cards. I don't think prayers are ever wasted. By staying in touch with the family I may be able to contribute somehow to the next generation and their growth in the Lord." Melissa rested her work in her lap.

"You don't actually get mail back from anyone, do you?" Angie's voice grew wistful. "All I get are advertisements." She showed Melissa the return address of a car dealer on her letter.

"I like feeling connected with my family even though I'm thousands of miles away surrounded by cattle and fir trees instead of relatives. I'm helping my own joy."

"I guess it was receiving only the usual junk mail that made me walk on over to your place. Do you think if I wrote someone in your family, they'd write me back?"

"I'll bet they would," Melissa answered, thinking, *I'll write to them first and tell them how much this isolated woman needs some mail.*

When Paul wrote to the Colossians, he used a phrase we often hear paraphrased. He wrote about being absent in the flesh but present in the spirit. That tie which joins our spirit with another person is worth establishing and maintaining.

⸻

GOD'S PATTERN

God is pleased when we make the effort to remain in
relationships with the people He plants in our lives.
We never know how our lives may impact people for Christ
because we have taken time for them. God can use even small,
infrequent contacts for good. Sometimes we may never know
how much our efforts mattered.

WHERE'S THE PENCIL?

*For I know the thoughts that I think
toward you, saith the LORD,
thoughts of peace, and not of evil,
to give you an expected end.*
JEREMIAH 29:11 KJV

*Where there is no vision, the people perish:
but he that keepeth the law, happy is he.*
PROVERBS 29:18 KJV

"Does that look like the right height?" Kevin asked his wife, hammering two nails in the wall and hanging a dowel rod on it.

"I'll put the quilt on the rod, and we'll see." Vicky hung her wall hanging by its loops, rested the dowel on the nails, and stepped back to survey the effect. A chuckle turned into giggles and quickly grew into laughter. "Quick, hold up the wall before the quilt pulls it into the cellar!" Vicky ran to the wall and pretended to hold it up.

"It does look a little lopsided," Kevin said, examining Vicky's face for any sign he shouldn't join in her merriment. After all, she had spent months making this quilt. He didn't want her to think he was laughing at it. But the more they looked, the funnier it became.

"All the dark colors are on one side and make it look like it's dragging the whole wall down." Vicky could hardly speak around her giggle attack.

"Are those two baskets of flowers supposed to be hanging upside down while the rest are face up?" Kevin asked.

"Oh, I never noticed that before." Vicky sobered.

"Never mind." Kevin put his arms around her. "I like it because you made it."

She hugged him back. "Thanks, but you don't have to. I enjoyed doing it, so I'll just make another one. But this time I'll do what everyone told me I should do in the first place. Plan ahead. Got a pencil? I'll draw this as it ought to look and mark where I could change the colors so it doesn't look unbalanced."

Gorgeous quilts require planning. The pattern choice needs to fit the level of skill we've developed. The selection of fabric requires forethought for a pleasing blend and arrangement. A diagram to guide the arrangement of pieces provides a good checkpoint as the work progresses.

If we take the time to plan for good results with a quilt project, think how much more God planned when He created us. Ask God to show us His plan and our role in advancing His kingdom on earth.

GOD'S PATTERN
God is an excellent planner.
His plans for us are designed for our good.
He has held the blueprint for our lives
from the moment of our conception.

A QUEENLY TASK

And David was greatly distressed;
for the people spake of stoning him,
because the soul of all the people was grieved,
every man for his sons and for his daughters:
but David encouraged himself in the LORD his God.
1 SAMUEL 30:6 KJV

S it quietly, Little Queen, and ply thy needle with diligence.
You must earn people's respect with your skills and self-control if you are to reign well." The words rang true, but the harsh tone the court noblewoman used nettled Mary, whose needlework lay on the ground where she had just thrown it.

Mary retrieved the offending material, tucked her black velvet slippers under her satin dress, and straightened in the gilded chair until she felt the heavy braid of her gown scratch her shoulders. She glared back at the lady in an effort not to cry. Whenever the sharp-nosed noble ladies corrected her during their handwork sessions, homesickness for her mother overwhelmed her. Her Scottish homeland never seemed farther away. In the year since she had come to the French court for her education, she had learned which of the noblewomen in the court were mean and cross. Everyone seemed to think she had the right to tell her how a queen should act.

"Do grown-ups ever grow tired of sitting so still?" Mary whispered into her tutor's ear.

"We've just learned to hide it better than seven-year-olds," the courtesan answered kindly. "Never you mind. These ladies are jealous because you were made a queen when you were only one month old; some of these old harpies will never be more than a countess or less." She covered her mouth with her embroidery hoop so no one could overhear.

"Look at the knots in my peacock," Mary groaned when her thread tangled. She returned to her work under the glare of a lady whose fluffy pink dress and perfect curls clashed with her grouchy disposition.

In spite of the stifling afternoons with the royal ladies, Mary Queen of Scots developed skill with her needle and came to find solace in her work, for she was lonely in her peculiar position as a child queen far from her throne and homeland. During the time of the Renaissance in France in the mid-1500s, elaborate needlework was important to the queens and noble-women, and Mary grew adept at plying her needle whether in embroidery, appliqué, or making charming tops for decorative coverlets, which were highly valued in the bedchamber.

When Mary returned to Scotland, court intrigue and tragedy filled her life. In danger, she fled to England for protection, only to find herself considered a suspect in plots against Queen Elizabeth. Virtually under house arrest in the home of the Earl of Shrewsbury, Mary once again sought the solace of creating beauty with her needle. She continued to turn to her craft for comfort when Elizabeth transferred her to prison before having her beheaded February 8, 1587. Some of the lovely things she made are displayed in Hardwick Hall.

Crafts are an excellent way to encourage ourselves when we are in difficult situations. They supply a useful way to discharge emotional tension. David had an even better way. The scripture in 1 Samuel tells us he turned to the Lord for encouragement. By praising God for His goodness and remembering the times when the Lord had helped him through previous troubles, David's faith increased until he was able to trust God with the current difficulty.

GOD'S PATTERN

God is with us in every trouble
and will help us find a way
to encourage ourselves.

YOU'RE OKAY

*To the praise of the glory of his grace,
wherein he hath made us accepted in the beloved.*
EPHESIANS 1:6 KJV

Brittany tightened her jaw as Hunter Mellon drove her into his parents' driveway. Brittany had met Hunter's mother only twice before for short, nervous visits. She twisted the diamond on her left hand and wondered if Mrs. Mellon liked her or not. Oh, their phone conversations were always cordial, and she enjoyed the cards Mrs. Mellon sent for holidays, but Brittany's insecurity lingered. Deep down, was she what Mrs. Mellon wanted for her son?

"Come on." Hunter took her hand to help her out of the car. "Mom hasn't bitten a girlfriend yet."

"But I'm more than a girlfriend now." She twisted the diamond again.

"You're gonna wear the ring out before we're married if you keep that up." Hunter propelled her up the steps with an arm around her waist.

"Dinner's nearly ready, dear," Mrs. Mellon said after a warm greeting. "Make yourself comfortable in the family room, and I'll bring you some fruit juice while the roast finishes cooking. The house rule is guests don't work until they've been here twenty-four hours. You're not a guest, Hunter, so you can come get the heavy platter from the top of the china cabinet."

Brittany looked around the room while she waited. A large

package was gift-wrapped in the corner. She could see a gift tag on it but could not read the name from her distance. Afraid to appear nosy, Brittany resisted the temptation to get up and look at it. Instead she looked at a quilted wall hanging filled with stylized cats beside her. An Autumn Leaf quilt was draped over the back of the sofa.

Mrs. Mellon brought in a tray with three glasses of cranberry juice. "What do you say we not wait until after dinner?" she asked Hunter as she set the drinks on the coffee table.

"Fine with me," Hunter said, "it's your present."

"I want you to know how glad we are that you're joining our family. I think this will speak for itself about our welcome to you." Mrs. Mellon picked up the big gift in the corner and set it on Brittany's lap.

Brittany tried to remain calm, but as soon as she removed the tape from one end of the gift she forgot decorum. Squealing, she tore the paper off with a big rip. "A quilt! Mrs. Mellon, did you make me a quilt? I can't believe you made me a quilt." She unfolded the Double Wedding Ring quilt. Hunter jumped up and helped her stretch it out for a full view. Each gold and blue ring contained a star medallion in the center.

"I can't imagine how many hours you had to work on this." Brittany blinked against the sting at the back of her eyes. She dropped her corner to turn toward Hunter's mother, who reached her arms out wide.

The tight little knot that had been lodged in Brittany's middle ever since she boarded the airplane for Denver that morning dissolved. The acceptance the quilt symbolized soothed her nerves, and she relaxed, knowing the family accepted her. For many years, the sacrifice of time and energy the quilt represented reminded Brittany of her in-laws' love and helped maintain a warm friendship between the two women.

God accepts us with rejoicing when we come to join His

family. He paid the ultimate price to make a way for us to become part of His family with the sacrifice of His life. Regardless of our insecurities and failures, God accepts us, flaws and all.

GOD'S PATTERN
We can extend the love and acceptance
we have received from our heavenly Father
to those around us so they can see
a tangible example of what God's love is like.

PRETTY PLEASE

A good man leaveth an inheritance
to his children's children:
and the wealth of the sinner
is laid up for the just.
PROVERBS 13:22 KJV

L ook. Grandma's label called this a Flying Geese quilt."

"Ooh, I like the crazy quilt. Feel the velvet."

"I should be the one who gets the Lone Star quilt. I'm from Texas."

"I didn't know Mother had finished so many quilts." Adrianne Lotts smiled as her children exclaimed over the quilts they found in their grandmother's cedar chest.

"There are enough here for each of us to pick out two. You should have first choice, Mother." Lora pulled her mother over to the chest. "Aren't they pretty?"

"Beautiful. I'll wait until you each pick the one you like best." Adrianne's eyes misted while she watched her children spread the quilts out over the furniture to admire. "I wish Grandma could see your excitement and appreciation about inheriting her quilts."

"Grandma was a sweetie. What better remembrance of her could we have than something she spent hours putting together?" Sherry ran her finger over the fabric roses curled into a wreath.

"This is the best inheritance. These quilts mean more to us than her jewelry. She invested something of herself in them.

They represent the essence of Grandma." Lori searched for a way to explain how much she valued the quilts.

"See, Mom, how happy Grandma made everybody. Now you know what you've gotta do," Ken said. "Take up quilt making so you can leave us an inheritance we can rave about."

"Seriously, Mom. I'll bet you would like making these as much as Grandma did. We'd love receiving them," Adrianne said.

"Make me one with pinks and magenta to match my bedroom. Quilts make the perfect keepsake," Lora added.

The more Adrianne thought about that morning and discovering the quilts, the more the idea of quilting took root in her mind. *After all*, she thought as she looked up the craft store in the phone book, *what else am I leaving my children that matters to them?*

Because parents love their children, they desire to leave them things of value that they hope will make the offspring remember them with fondness. As lovely and precious as some of our possessions may be, we have a far better inheritance to leave our children. We have the power to leave our children with an example of relating to God that will impact them the rest of their lives. "I pray also that the eyes of your heart may be enlightened in order that you may know the hope to which he has called you, the riches of his glorious inheritance in the saints" (Ephesians 1:18 NIV).

GOD'S PATTERN

God instructs us to leave our children an inheritance.
His desire extends beyond leaving behind material things.
He wants us to leave our children with a hunger to know God better and a passion to love and serve Him.

A FERVENT SOLDIER

Not slothful in business;
fervent in spirit; serving the Lord.
ROMANS 12:11 KJV

I've never met a hero before," Lisbet said, pulling on her newest dress. She enjoyed the rustle of the blue taffeta as it settled over her hoop underskirt.

"You'll meet a real hero when you meet Marquis de Lafayette at the banquet tonight." Mother stood behind Lisbet with the buttonhook ready to pull the long row of tiny buttons through their buttonholes. "We might have lost the Revolutionary War without the Marquis' help. He used his youthful energy and much of his French wealth to help America win its independence from England. I remember how thankful I felt when his efforts forced Cornwallis to surrender. After that, in 1781, my brothers were able to come home from the war."

"I'm so excited Philadelphia decided to honor his American visit that I can hardly tie the ribbon in my hair." Lisbet held her ribbon out to her mother for help.

"Even though it's now 1824, those of us who worried and prayed about the birth of our nation wouldn't forget to honor a fervent soldier like the Marquis de Lafayette."

The clop of the horses' hooves bringing the carriage to their door stopped their conversation, and Lisbet and Mother hastened downstairs.

To Lisbet's delight she was seated near the Marquis de Lafayette at the feast. In her eagerness not to miss a word he said, she scarcely remembered to eat. She learned a lot listening to the tall man reminisce about serving on George Washington's staff without pay and how he'd spent part of a miserable winter in Valley Forge. When the dessert was served, Lafayette chose an orange. Lisbet watched with fascination when he took his knife and scored the rind of the fruit into four equal parts before carefully peeling them back. Lisbet surprised herself when she spoke up before he began to section the neatly peeled orange. "Please, sir, may I have your orange peel?" After a startled glance at her, the Marquis handed her the four neat pieces of peel.

When she reached home, she unwrapped them from her handkerchief and placed them on a table with their four corners coming together to form a point in the middle. "Look, mother what a pretty quilt pattern this will make. I'll find materials in blue and red to remember our American Revolution hero."

Because American women felt immense gratitude for the Marquis de Lafayette, the pattern became very popular. Many quilts were made using this design with a wide variety of colors. Because the pattern followed the curved line of the orange peel, beginning quilters usually did not try it.

Marquis de Lafayette's fervent help propelled the ragged American army to victory over the polished English army. As soldiers in God's army, we need to exhibit the same fervor. The slothful never win wars. We are engaged in a war to win others to Christ, to overcome worldly temptations in our lives, and to become more and more like Christ. A hero inspires us to emulate him. When we fervently serve our Lord, others may see the victory of Christ in our lives and feel inspired to join God's army.

GOD'S PATTERN

Just as the repetition of a pattern makes an attractive quilt,
a life well lived inspires others to repeat the proven pattern.

WORK IN PROGRESS

For by him were all things created,
that are in heaven, and that are in earth,
visible and invisible, whether they be thrones,
or dominions, or principalities, or powers:
all things were created by him, and for him.
COLOSSIANS 1:16 KJV

Rachel peered into her mother's sewing basket. "We only have light-colored thread. How are we going to sew Noah's Ark and the dark-colored animals on the quilt for Edie's baby?" Rachel asked her mother as she helped cut out two giraffes from a worn-out dress. "Is anyone driving the horse and wagon into town for supplies?"

"No, but it wouldn't do any good if we did. The last time I went to the store, there weren't any dark-colored threads, and the shopkeeper assured me he didn't get them in very often. We're going to unravel Pa's old shirt." Mother emptied her ragbag on a chair. "He has a brown and a gray shirt too worn-out on the elbows and the front to wear." She held them up to examine. "The backs are good. I'd appreciate your help unraveling while I set the bread to rise." Mother put the shirts on the table, snipped the bottom hem off, and began to carefully pull on the bottom thread, loosening it from the shirt and winding it onto an old wooden spool.

"I'd rather set the bread," Rachel said. "Not breaking the threads when I pull is slow work."

"That's fine with me. My legs are ready to sit." Mother

pulled up a chair and continued drawing the threads loose from the fabric of the shirt.

"Your sister will love the animals you outlined from the pictures in the big family Bible for her baby's quilt."

"But Edie's so picky she won't like it if our stitches show because we've sewn with the wrong color of thread."

In the early days on our nation's frontier, matching thread to fabric was more of a challenge than it is today when manufacturers produce a wide variety of colors. We are careful to match the thread to the fabric we're sewing so it isn't noticeable. The thread itself is a thin tool but makes a strong bond between two pieces of fabric. Likewise, quilting thread is nearly invisible as we stitch our patterns with it. But the tiny crevice it creates as it draws the three layers of a quilt together forms puffs of design that are pleasing to our eyes.

By itself a stitch is insignificant, but line up stitch upon stitch and the result is attractive or practical. In the same way, the Lord works with us, a stitch at a time.

GOD'S PATTERN

Often God's work is invisible on the outside because
He is stitching on the inside first. We must exert patience
with one another because we are works in progress.
He establishes the proper pace to work with each person.
Sometimes it is slower than what we would select,
but when He is done, the accomplishment
will serve His purpose well.

RAFFLE FOR LIFE

I'm sorry, but neither you nor your husband is a match for Tammy's bone marrow transplant." Dr. Hobart averted his eyes from Robin's face instead of watching it crumple into tears.

"We have other recourses. I've contacted the Red Cross, and they're checking their databases for volunteer bone marrow donors. Perhaps they'll have a match for Tammy. We need matches on at least six markers to make the transplant a good risk." Dr. Hobart sat down in a chair across from Robin. He hated the days when he couldn't offer instant hope to parents of children like Tammy. He had a two-year-old at home, the same age as Tammy, and he couldn't imagine facing the terrors of leukemia. This was one of those days he wondered why he ever studied medicine.

"You might find a match among relatives or friends if you have people who are willing to undergo the test and put their names on our volunteer files. Occasionally people balk at paying the sixty-five dollars to suffer a needle stick for their blood, but many are willing. It costs even more if they only want to donate to a specific person and not go on our donor list. Sometimes organizations raise the money to pay for the tests, allowing the family to round up a lot of people for the tissue typing."

Robin's emotions were still swirling when she walked into her house late the same evening. Her husband, Alex, had already left for his second job. The red light on her telephone answering machine was blinking. She kicked off her shoes, punched the replay button, and flopped into a chair, too tired to move. The monotone voice of her dentist's secretary reminded her of her checkup. She'd have to call and cancel; she wasn't going to leave Tammy alone in the hospital for that. A chimney sweep offered a discount to clean her chimney for winter.

At the third message, she bolted upright and grabbed a pencil. The president of her quilt guild was offering to hold a quilt raffle to raise money. Each guild in the region volunteered to donate a quilt for the cause. The president had heard Tammy needed a bone marrow transplant and wondered if the family needed money to attract a large number of possible donors to do the tissue typing. Robin scribbled the number down, and pent-up tears flowed. Hope soared, recharging her energy bank. "Thank You, God, thank You."

Hope brings strength and restores our ability to persevere in difficult circumstances. When confronted with challenging situations, people often need help to cling to meager portions of hope. By offering our resources of emotional and tangible support, we offer hope to people. God offers the best hope because He is an everlasting source of mercy.

GOD'S PATTERN

God is pleased when we find ways to bring hope to discouraged
people. Pointing people toward scriptures that show
the goodness of God brings hope to people.
When our hope is founded upon the mercy of God,
our hope is planted on a firm foundation. "Let thy mercy,
O LORD, be upon us, according as we hope in thee."
PSALM 33:22 KJV

Thy Rod and Staff and Quilt

Yea, though I walk through
the valley of the shadow of death,
I will fear no evil:
for thou art with me;
thy rod and thy staff they comfort me.
PSALM 23:4 KJV

L isten to us. We're buzzing louder than a beehive." Rosa spoke over the conversation of fifteen women whose tongues had no trouble keeping up with their needles as they finished up the thirty crib-size quilts they were making.

"At least we're as productive as a beehive. We've made a lot of beautiful quilts." Maria gestured to the growing pile of finished quilts folded and ready for them to deliver to the children's hospital after lunch.

Rosa had the forethought to tuck several packets of tissue into her purse before they went to the cancer ward of the hospital where they moved through the beds, handing a brightly colored quilt to each of the children. Some sat up in eager anticipation, and some were too sick to do more than clutch their gift. As the afternoon wore on, the quilters talked to the patients and some of their parents, often crying unabashedly with them.

When Dr. Long made an unscheduled visit to check on some of the children, he had trouble getting to tummies and chests to listen to abdomens and heartbeats. He kept folding quilts out of the way, only to have them drawn back into determined arms.

Susie was particularly stubborn. She would not let go of her quilt for the doctor to look at the intravenous needle in her hand. Instead she drew him into a prolonged conversation about the bright colors.

"The doctor is not going to appreciate us after Susie eats up his valuable time," Rosa whispered to the head nurse.

"On the contrary," the nurse replied, "he probably wants to do cartwheels through the ward. No one has been able to get two sentences in a row out of Susie since she came. She's had some painful treatments and drew into a silent world of her own. This is the most I've seen her communicate."

When Maria discovered many children lived too far away for their families to visit often, she gathered up storybooks from the hospital playroom, and each woman cuddled a lonely child for a time of entertaining tales well mixed with individual attention.

The ward rang with protests when it was time for the guild to leave. Several women decided they would return to play with the children again. Those women kept the rest of the quilt guild informed about how each child progressed. Together they cried when a child died. They rejoiced and sent welcome home cards to those who had bone marrow transplants and recovered.

The whole group trooped over once more to celebrate when Susie was well enough to go home, still clutching her bright rainbow quilt.

Although the reason is hard to explain, people find comfort in handmade quilts. Perhaps it's because they are attractive and warm. Maybe knowing someone took trouble and time for us forms part of the appeal. More than any quilt, God is available to comfort us in our difficulties and sorrows. He will wrap us in His love when we ask.

GOD'S PATTERN

In biblical times the rod referred to
in Psalm 23 was a symbol of authority.
The staff was used as support for climbing
and to scare predators away from sheep.
We rest in comfort when we call on God's rod of
authority and staff of protection in any situation.
God's comfort is available to us for every need.
Sometimes He will use people to comfort us,
and sometimes He will whisper comfort
into our hearts if we listen.

QUILTING AT PERIL

But I say unto you,
Love your enemies, bless them that curse you,
do good to them that hate you,
and pray for them which despitefully use you,
and persecute you.
MATTHEW 5:44 KJV

With a flourish of satisfaction, Anita pulled through the final stitch attaching snow to the top of her rendition of the Andes mountains. They formed a pretty background for her wall quilt. Next, she secured a golden sun above the mountains to remind her of God's warmth and the hope His Bible promises offered.

"I'm going to believe Your promises, God, no matter how much I lack in my life," Anita murmured in determination as she stitched.

"Help me forgive the men who have my husband, whoever they are, and please take care of my Ramon wherever he is and keep him from harm." Without thinking of the other women stitching in the church hall, she prayed softly, a habit she developed while she worked on her politically pointed needlework. To her delight, the women joined in agreement with her prayer and added the names of their beloved men.

Through the church window the sight of the real Andes loomed over the city of Santiago, Chile. The view of the solid mountain glowing in the light of the setting sun brought reassurance to her. With each change in the position of the sun, the mountain took on a different hue; but it remained a dependable sight, never moving or disappearing in spite of the chaos in its shadow. Anita laid her *arpilleras* appliqué in her lap to soak in the majestic sight. She willed herself to look up over the deteriorating neighborhood around her. The buildings shrieked poverty and oppression. Even the burlap backing of her quilt, which gave the embroidery its name, *arpilleras,* testified to the scarcity of money for materials.

With a sigh Anita picked up her work again. "I've heard the regime is angry about these pictures we embroider. They don't like the church selling them to the world outside because they reveal the government repression."

"And how do the authorities expect us to eat with our husbands on the Detained and Disappeared list except we turn our needles to earn a little income?" Sophia looked up from her stitchery. "Who knows if our men live or if they're already murdered?"

Anita began to form a figure bringing a whip down on a laborer's back in the foreground of her work. "If I die for my picture, then I die," she said. "Better to die making a statement than to merely dwindle away in starvation." Anita clapped her hand over the rumble of her stomach stimulated by the aroma of the soup pot simmering in the church kitchen.

Sophia laughed when her own middle gave an answering rumble. "I'm weary of the struggle for enough food. I do well to remember to stay thankful for our church organizing a way to sell our work."

Anita looked around the room. Every face reflected the sadness of her heart. She wondered if the foreigner she hoped would buy her picture would understand the dreadful repression that clouded the life of its creator. Worn down with fear and want, she applied her energies to the only way she knew to protest against repression.

"Justice for all" she embroidered at the bottom. As she stitched, she prayed, "God, Your Word says, 'Love your enemies.' I can't do it except You give me the grace and Your love for the people."

"The same for me," Sophia prayed beside her, hoping her work presented a strong enough message to spur other countries into applying pressure on her government to improve its ways.

The sale of *arpilleras* stitchery has brought pressure on the Chilean government for change and hope into the hearts of women.

GOD'S PATTERN

God requires us to forgive those who persecute us.
Because this runs contrary to human nature,
we must ask Him to help us become
willing and able to forgive those
who have harmed us.

CAT CLAWS
AND PIG SQUEALS

Give not that which is holy unto the dogs,
neither cast ye your pearls before swine,
lest they trample them under their feet,
and turn again and rend you.
MATTHEW 7:6 KJV

C ome see the baby pigs," Rosy greeted her mother, Jessica, when she got out of her car. "They're one week old today. Go on around; I'll join you as soon as I round up the bread dough."

Jessica walked around the house to the pigpen, where she stopped in her tracks and stared. Her granddaughter, Grace, sat cross-legged on the ground outside the pen holding a squealing piglet wrapped in a quilt, in her quilt—the Circular Saw quilt. *Why, the very idea.* It had taken her forever to piece all those little sawtooth triangles.

"Do you have any idea how many times I ripped out and resewed to get those circular pieces to fit together?" Jessica loomed over her granddaughter.

"What circles?" Grace looked to both sides and then behind her in bewilderment.

"These curved lines right here." Jessica grabbed the quilt and snatched it into her arms, flipping the pink piglet onto the ground, where it took off squealing for its mother.

"Grandma, don't hurt the piggy."

"Don't hurt my quilt." Jessica shook it and leaned close to examine it for damage.

"Look. Mud stains on my quilt. Where's your appreciation of fine things?"

She turned toward the house to tell her daughter about the sacrilege to her quilt when her eye fell on the tent her granddaughters had strung in the backyard with the Victoria's Crown cover she had made and given to Rosy.

"Have you no respect?"

At the sound of her grandmother's shout, Grace's sister lifted the flap of the quilt and crawled out to see the reason for the racket.

"Did you make holes in my quilt with those stakes?" Jessica stalked over to examine the corners where sticks lay as weights.

"What's going on?" Rosy walked down the back steps.

"Your girls are mistreating my quilts. Why, Grace actually wrapped a pig in my Circular Saw quilt." She jabbed the air in the direction of the pigpen. "Don't they have any idea how valuable a handmade quilt is?"

Rosy laughed. "Mother, I have a friend who makes quilts explicitly for her cat and her dog. She keeps several around for them to sleep on."

"She can cast her pearls before swine if she wants, but I don't make quilts for pigs." Rosy thought she almost could hear the air crackle with hostility as Jessica marched into the house carrying the Circular Saw quilt with her.

Jessica's investment of herself into her quilts caused her to lose track of her priorities. Her relationship with her daughter and granddaughters carried infinitely more value than a quilt. Harmony between people surpasses material possessions in its ability to bring satisfaction and joy. No material item, regardless of its worth or sentimental value, is worth the loss of happy relationships. When the scripture speaks about casting our pearls before swine, it refers to the holy gospel. If people refuse to hear and believe in the gospel, but rather scorn and degrade it, we do well to avoid a combative approach. Instead, by continuing to demonstrate love for the people, their spirits may soften toward God. If we wait for God to work a readiness in their hearts before we continue hammering them with scripture verses, we may experience the joy of seeing them believe.

GOD'S PATTERN
Honor God's Word by not
submitting it to scorn and derision.

OUR FIRE CHIEF

When thou passest through the waters,
I will be with thee; and through the rivers,
they shall not overflow thee:
when thou walkest through the fire,
thou shalt not be burned;
neither shall the flame kindle upon thee.
ISAIAH 43:2 KJV

Shin dragged himself into his home in Tokyo, Japan. Shaky from exhaustion mixed with shock, he could hardly remove his shoes at the door.

Hoshi's eyes widened when she looked at her husband. "Your jacket and your trousers are burned. Are you hurt?" Running to her husband, Hoshi ran her fingers along the edges of the large gaps in his *sashiko*-stitched firefighter jacket. Tufts of blackened batting poked out of many holes.

"I'm better than I would have been without this outfit you made me." Shin tried to pull the damaged jacket over his head. He winced when Hoshi grabbed his arm.

"Sit down. You look faint." Hoshi helped him sink onto a mat. "You're hurt." Her voice rose after she pulled his jacket off. Patches of burns dotted his back where the fire had penetrated his thick, quilted clothes.

"I'm grateful you quilted my garment or think how much worse my injuries. . ." His voice trailed off as he took her hand. "I've never taken the time to thank you for the hours you stitched to make my fire clothes."

Hoshi bowed her head, remembering how often she had wearied of making the same running stitches over and over through the layers of heavy fabric. She contrived pleasant curves to break the monotony, but only her love for her husband had kept her at the task.

"Did you soak your garments in water long enough before going into the fire?" Hoshi carried her pot of healing salve to the mat.

"Yes, and several times I left the building to soak down again. See how dry the cloth is? The heat from the fire quickly evaporated the water. If I had left to wet myself down one more time, maybe my jacket wouldn't have begun to smolder. But I stayed longer to find the couple's little boy. He was so afraid he hid." Shin moaned at her touch in spite of her gentle hands. "It feels as if you're stabbing me with your needle."

"That's appropriate since my stitchery is called *sashiko*, meaning little stabs." Hoshi babbled on, trying to distract him. "I made plenty of stabs before finishing your firefighter outfit."

Shin tried to stifle his groans. "Father will call me a coward."

When she finished applying the soothing cream to the burned places, she continued to stroke his head until he fell into an exhausted sleep. She wished she could protect his heart as easily as she made the firefighter outfit to protect his body. Quilted fabric, no matter how thick, couldn't protect him from the daily barbs his father threw at him. Many cloth layers sewn together and drenched in water slowed fire and flames from scorching his skin, but no amount of water quenched the burns his father's harsh tongue inflicted on his soul.

Around three hundred years ago, especially in the Japanese countryside, the art of *sashiko* was developed to hold several cloth layers together for warm clothes and to protect firemen. God's love insulates us when we feel the flames of trials singe our lives.

When we are drenched with His love, trying circumstances are unable to kindle our emotions into a fire that burns out of control. The scorch of difficulties can't overcome us.

GOD'S PATTERN
Soak in His love to absorb
a protective layer against life's difficulties
and to prevent burns from fiery trials.

SANDPAPER

As iron sharpens iron,
so one man sharpens another.
PROVERBS 27:17 NIV

Abby's front door opened, admitting her next-door neighbor along with a strong breeze. Abby leaned over to retrieve the plastic template the wind blew on the floor. "This quilt pattern is driving me crazy. The slightest thing knocks it out of place."

Phyllis pranced in without waiting for an invitation. "I've got time between laundry loads so I thought I'd come fill your ear with the latest troubles in the neighborhood. What are you doing?"

"I'm trying to finish cutting out these diamond shapes for my Lone Star quilt, but this slick plastic pattern keeps shifting all over the place. I need to cut the pieces exactly right or the star will come out funny."

When Phyllis drew out a chair and settled into it as if she was there to stay, Abby added, "I'm going to have to stop in a few minutes to go to the grocery." *Forgive me, Lord, but it's not a complete lie. I do have to go to the grocery, just not in a few minutes.*

Undeterred, Phyllis was off and babbling about her latest woe, a complaint over her neighbor's dog ruining her tomato plants.

Abby swallowed a sigh. She knew the woman was lonely since her husband died last February, but her steady stream of grumbling wore on Abby's patience. Her mind wandered as she continued to cut, but Phyllis's next topic snapped Abby back to attention.

"I miss George. Seems like I can't get myself back on the right track since he died; you know, like church and God and all. He knew how to make light of aggravations; and before I knew it, he'd have me laughing." But it was tears that hovered around her eyes now.

God, forgive me for failing this woman. Show me how I can help. Abby set her scissors down and reached out to pat Phyllis's arm. "I'm sorry," she said, but she meant a whole lot more.

"Your pattern skittered out of place again." Phyllis changed the subject to cover her emotion. "I know a trick to help. Got a piece of sandpaper?"

"Sandpaper?" Had her neighbor finally flipped in her grief? Chagrined because she had avoided rather than helped her neighbor, she walked to the utility room and pulled out a sheet of sandpaper from her husband's tool chest.

Phyllis traced the diamond shape on the back of the sandpaper and cut it out. "There." She handed the pattern to Abby. "Put the rough side down on the fabric, and it will cling to the material and stay put."

"Wonderful!" Abby's voice lilted with genuine delight. She hugged Phyllis. "You've saved my sanity."

"What are neighbors for?" Phyllis returned the hug. "My mother taught me that trick. She was always quilting. Maybe I ought to get into making quilts again. Do you think it'd help me feel better?"

The rough edges of our personalities often grate on one another. Sometimes they seem like sandpaper roughing up our lives. The natural tendency is to pull away and avoid the irritation. If, instead, we allow God to use the irritant to reveal areas in our character where He wants to smooth us and make us into a polished person, we can tolerate the aggravating aspects of others.

By concentrating on the benefits of their acquaintance, we can build healthy bonds and flourish in His way.

GOD'S PATTERN

God uses the rough edges of
irritating people to shape and cut us
into a pattern making us
more like Jesus Christ.

SMELLS GOOD

"Thanks for all the fun, Granddad. The best part of my visit was tromping through the woods to cut our Christmas tree. Come see us soon." Cheri's husband gave the car horn a toot. "Hate to say good-bye." Cheri threw her arms around her grandfather and buried her head in his chest. She breathed deeply of the scent of wood smoke that clung to his clothes. "You smell good, like the woodstove. Makes me wish I had one in our apartment."

"You best get movin'. Don't want you driving home in the dark." Granddad patted her back and walked her to the car.

"Happy New Year," Cheri called out the window as they drove off.

Early in January, Cheri's mother, Rhea, called with the sad news. Granddad had died. "Died peacefully in his sleep," Rhea said. Together Cheri and Rhea packed and cleaned his little mountain cabin.

"Here, I'll open the door." Cheri twisted the latch and opened the firebox for the log her mother carried. "I helped Granddad keep the fire going when Charles and I were here for Christmas. I love its smell. All of Granddad's flannel shirts carry the aroma." Cheri held to her nose the pile of shirts she carried. "Doesn't the woodstove odor make you remember him?"

"What are we going to do with those old flannel shirts?" Rhea asked.

"I know what to do. I'll make a quilt out of them. Then I'll always have the scent of Granddad in the house."

Cheri followed through on her thought. She made a quilt of her grandfather's shirts, cut with a pocket centered in each square. Finished, it gave a rugged, woodsy touch to her wood-beamed family room. For years, the aroma of a wood fire lingered in the material; and whenever she sank her face into the quilt folds, she remembered her granddad.

When we have given our heart and life to Jesus, the Lord savors our aroma. Isn't it amazing to think we smell good to God? He enjoys the scent of our life lived here on earth for Him.

GOD'S PATTERN
Our love of God gives us a pleasant scent.
Without being aware of it,
both the saved and
the unsaved sense our aroma.

FOLLOW ME

The Lord Jesus Christ, who,
by the power that enables him to
bring everything under his control,
will transform our lowly bodies so that
they will be like his glorious body.
PHILIPPIANS 3:20–21 NIV

I admit I like the idea of appliquéing sunbonnet girls for my granddaughters, but then I look at all those fancy curlicues you stitch on your quilts, and I give up the idea of ever making a quilt." Donna resisted her friend's suggestion that she begin quilting.

"You don't have to do all that patterned stitching. I'll teach you to do echo quilting instead." Joy was persistent.

"What's that?" Donna sounded doubtful.

"It's easy, I promise. You get a sunbonnet girl ready, and I'll show you how."

Donna loved selecting pieces of the fabrics she had used for her granddaughters' clothes when they were smaller. With big sunbonnets perched on top of cone-shaped dresses, she didn't have to worry about shaping heads or faces. In short order, she had the first square ready.

"Finally, I've a friend I can sit and sew with while we chat," Joy said when Donna came to learn the quilting.

"Bet you get tired of trying to teach my clumsy fingers."

"I'll teach you quilting, and you teach me patience with teenagers. Bet you didn't think I noticed, but you're a good example with your kids which I need to follow."

"Does it matter if I get this second row of stitching exactly one quarter of an inch away from the first?" Donna interrupted their conversation to ask after she had sewed the first row of stitches close to the fabric of the sunbonnet girl all the way around.

"I just estimate when I do it. But if you want to make it even, use a ruler and mark the distance with a washable marker."

"You win. Echo stitching is easy," Donna said when she completed the square. "Is that all I do?"

"You'll do the same echo stitching along the strips you sew between your squares. Lots of quilting makes the fabric stay flat and sturdy, but if it's the appliquéing you enjoy, what you're doing is plenty. That's the nice part of quilting. You make the project as simple or as complicated as you wish."

In echo quilting, the first line of stitching provides the guideline for each succeeding line of stitches. The second row follows the path the first row established by a distance of either one-fourth or one-eighth inch. In our Christian walk, we try to follow the path our Lord Jesus set for us when He walked on the earth. Our goal is to become like Him in our thinking, our actions, and our reactions. If we study what He did and how He did it, we have a guideline to follow. We also know people who live fine Christian lives and are examples worth following.

GOD'S PATTERN
When we pattern ourselves
more and more like our Savior,
our lives become an example and
an inspiration for others as they work
toward their goal of being like Jesus.

WHEN WE ARE ABSENT

The LORD watch between me and thee,
when we are absent one from another.
GENESIS 31:49 KJV

"Have another helping of apple cobbler." Wendy passed the pan to Gina. "I'm going to miss our dinners together."

"Me, too. Maybe I'm getting too old for moving. Saying good-bye keeps getting harder, although we're glad about Glen's promotion." Gina spooned a chunk of golden crust onto her plate and then passed the dish to her husband. "I'll miss coming to your house, looking at your Acorn quilt over your table. . .and spilling coffee on your floor," she added, dropping her paper napkin on the linoleum to soak up the liquid she sloshed from her cup when she gestured toward the quilt with her cup.

Everyone laughed.

"We need to go," Glen said, pushing his chair back. "The moving van is arriving at the crack of dawn tomorrow."

Gina stayed seated staring up at the quilt hanging over the kitchen table. "You make the prettiest quilts. I love the way each tree is different. I never got around to asking you to teach me how to quilt. I'm going to miss you so much."

"This is the next best thing to making a quilt together." Wendy climbed on a chair and lifted the quilt bar off the wall brackets. She slipped the quilt off the rod and dropped it down to Gina. "Take this with you and hang it in your Arizona kitchen to remind you of me and North Carolina oak trees."

"You don't really mean to give me your quilt." Gina held

it out to her friend. "You worked too hard on it to just give it away."

"You always examine it every time you come over. I love the idea you'll have it to remind you of me. Stop dripping tears on it. You'll start me crying, too." Wendy jumped from the chair. Caught in their hug, the quilt absorbed the tears.

Concrete reminders of friends and family help us deal with separation. Pictures and gifts form tangible ties that bring comfort. The effort to provide gifts, letters, and phone calls in order to maintain contact when we are apart speaks of the importance of one person to the other. These actions bless us because they testify that distance doesn't dim our love.

More important, the knowledge of God's power to watch over the absent loved ones enables us to endure separation. When we pray, committing the loved one to God's care, we are able to rest in His peace. He grants us insights into preserving long-distance relationships.

GOD'S PATTERN
Distance is not a barrier to God.
Through prayer we lift up our friends and family
for His blessings and care.

STURDY

*And wisdom and knowledge shall be
the stability of thy times,
and strength of salvation:
the fear of the LORD is his treasure.*
ISAIAH 33:6 KJV

I don't know what to do," Leslie confided to her sister, Joanne, as they worked on their quilt entry for the local fair. "Hal wants me to stay home when he goes to Richmond to hang our neighbor Jim's one-man show in the art museum. He thinks I'll serve a better purpose answering the phone here since our number is in the ad for the exhibit and loads of people will want information on how to find the museum. I'd much rather go to Richmond and get in on the excitement."

Leslie's eyes sparkled. "This is a major achievement for Jim, and Hal gets to stand around, talking to the people about his work, listening to the visitors' comments, and seeing all the other exciting exhibits. I get to stay home and instruct faceless phone voices where to turn left and when to turn right."

"Bummer," Joanne agreed.

"Mom! Guess what!" The slam of the screen door sounded at the same time Eddie skidded around the corner into the family room. "Coach said I'm a good backer."

"I'm glad your coach is pleased." Leslie looked over the quilting frame at her breathless son. "Exactly what is a 'backer'?"

"It's when I run like crazy from my place in the outfield and get near the second baseman in case he misses the ball. I did it. I snagged the ball and got it to first before the runner. He was out!" Eddie put his fist into the air and pulled it down as if he were pulling a cord of victory.

Leslie resisted the urge to cover her ears against Eddie's volume.

"Be glad his coach is free with his compliments," Joanne said as Eddie ricocheted off the doorjamb and out of the room to tell his brother about his triumph. "Brady's coach will only praise the ones who get the long hits and make the runs. He'd never praise someone for good backing."

"Makes me think of this quilt we're making. We took the time to put written history on the back; but probably everyone will pay attention to the picture on the front and not even notice the work we did on the back." Leslie shrugged.

"No matter, the back is important. It's what provides the stability for the quilt. The padding would be gone in no time without it."

Leslie clapped her hand to her cheek. "Listen to us. Why didn't I take that attitude in the first place? Of course the back of a quilt is important even if no one looks at it. Not everyone hits the winning run in a baseball game, and I can't measure and hammer nails for the art collection like Hal. But I can do like Eddie and be a good backer. Excuse me a minute. I'm going to call my husband and tell him I'm glad to stay home on the telephone and give directions to the museum."

Quilts, by definition, consist of more than one material layer. Although most quilts are backed with solid fabric, patterned material makes an attractive backing. Sheets or blankets back some quilts. The backing is often cut four or more inches larger than the quilt in order to fold the extra fabric over and form a border when it is stitched to the front.

Staying in the background to provide stability lacks glamour. By backing one another up in our endeavors and our emotions, we create stability. With the backing of friends, we can accomplish more than our abilities would achieve by themselves. Whether it is with resources, money, or simply emotional uplifting, we need the support of others. Spiritually we need the backing of each other when we face temptations or discouragement.

GOD'S PATTERN

God stands ready to back us up with His support.
We only need to whisper a cry for His help.

GOING ON

And he took bread, and gave thanks,
and brake it, and gave unto them, saying,
This is my body which is given for you:
this do in remembrance of me.
LUKE 22:19 KJV

I can't seem to help myself. I stay glued to the TV all day long. Part of me is so sickened by the carnage in Oklahoma City I hate to look, and another part of me keeps wanting to know every detail, as if learning more will somehow help me." Nan brought her portable TV to her quilt guild where the women watched the Oklahoma City bombing news coverage while they stitched. On this April 1995 day, their needles lay still more than they flashed.

"Those poor people! Makes me feel helpless seeing the suffering," Deedee said.

"I wish somehow I could get it behind me and go on with life. Look. There's that poor little baby again. Since the bombing wiped out the federal building, it seems like the TV station has shown the scene of the fireman carrying out the same child at least a hundred times." Nan turned her head away from the screen.

"I know, and I cry every time." Deb wiped her eyes. "I can't seem to stop crying."

"If we can't put it behind us here in North Carolina, think how long this will haunt the people in Oklahoma City."

"Forever!" Nan blew her nose. "Why don't we make a quilt in

honor of the victims? There's something healing about making a quilt when I'm grieving."

Deb pulled another tissue from the box. "What would we do with it? I think having it around the house would depress me."

"I'll fly it to Oklahoma City."

"Nan, you've never flown in an airplane in your life," Deedee objected.

"This might be what it takes to get me started. I think knowing people way out in North Carolina care that they lost loved ones would comfort families. Maybe a museum will show interest because someone cared."

All over the world people reacted in shocked horror at the senseless loss of 169 lives in the bombing of the federal building in Oklahoma City. Quilters turned to their craft for comfort from their grief and in an effort to convey sympathy for a tragedy that defied a way to find adequate expression. Groups from Pennsylvania to Massachusetts to places in Europe poured their anguish into quilts. One lady made nineteen quilts, one to honor each child lost in the bombing. Another named her king-size quilt the Bombing Memorial, and three hundred people from across the United States contributed to it. For one quilt, a photo of each bombing victim was photocopied onto material and used as the border around the piece. Connected through the Internet, people from around the world made a small wall hanging for each family of the victims.

Cross-stitched or embroidered squares made up one enormous quilt. Several displays of quilts traveled around the United States. One group of work, designed and sewed by professional artists, toured the United States for three years.

A museum curator reports that every tragedy of large proportions is greeted with an outpouring of quilts made to honor the victims. From plane crashes and school calamities to natural disasters, women find catharsis in memorializing the events with quilts. Creating a remembrance helps us deal with pain. God ordained a way to remember the ultimate sacrifice of His Son, Jesus, on the cross—Communion. When we partake of the bread and the wine or juice, we remember the suffering of our Savior in order that we might obtain forgiveness. While our minds cringe at the ordeal Jesus endured, our hearts rejoice because He secured eternal life for us. When we finish our life on earth, we will join our Lord and sing His praises for all eternity.

GOD'S PATTERN
Communion helps us remember with grateful,
rejoicing hearts the depth of the sacrifice
of Jesus Christ for us.

BANNER OF JOY

Lift ye up a banner upon the high mountain,
exalt the voice unto them, shake the hand,
that they may go into the gates of the nobles.
ISAIAH 13:2 KJV

Valerie looked around at the monthly meeting of the navy wives. Despondency lined the faces of the women. She felt responsible as the wife of the commander of the aircraft carrier. As they met, it was churning across the ocean bearing these women's husbands to the latest hot spot on the world's political scene.

"Even the sun hides behind the clouds today," a woman spoke over the murmur of voices.

Another expressed the gloom the women felt. "Fits my mood perfectly."

Now what do I do? Valerie thought. *There's no manual with a procedure for despair.*

Then she remembered her morning Bible reading about lifting up a banner on a mountain.

"Listen to my idea, gals. We need to switch our focus from how sad we feel because our husbands are gone to how glad we'll be when they return. Let's make a huge welcome home quilt to hang when they come steaming back into port."

The babble of voices crescendoed and an air of excitement filtered into the midst of the women, forcing dark moods away.

"I move we adopt Valerie's idea and make a welcome quilt," one voice rang out over the others.

"The bigger the better," another called.

The women wholeheartedly put their lonely energies into the project. Some learned to quilt for the first time from others practiced in the craft.

Some days Valerie almost regretted her suggestion. The coordination to involve as many spouses as possible in the effort challenged her organizational skills. She felt rewarded each time the women gathered to work on their blocks, and she watched active hands contribute to happy faces. The quilt provided an activity to keep the wives busy and contributed to their emotional stability while they waited for their men. With the women's minds absorbed preparing and anticipating the grand welcome home, the days passed more quickly.

As the weeks turned into months, the size of the quilt mushroomed, and Valerie enlisted the help of the base commander for assistance about how and where to hang the giant banner for the ship's homecoming.

The magic ability of a quilt to convey love and caring blanketed the ship's hangar deck with its warm embrace when the men saw the welcoming quilt hung on the side of a building beyond the ship's berth.

Our lives can become a banner that conveys our joy to the world. People feel the welcoming love of God when our facial expression, our words, and our actions advertise our love for God. His unconditional love for us amazes us and wreaths our souls with joy. The world packages many activities in the name of fun to attract us, but the joy of the Lord is a magnet with a powerful pull. Ask God to help us lift up our joy and let it shine in order to draw the world to Jesus Christ.

GOD'S PATTERN

God is the designer of joy, and He enjoys bestowing it on us.
He also uses it as a hook to attract people to His Good News.

STUFFED

May be able to comprehend with
all saints what is the breadth,
and length, and depth, and height;
And to know the love of Christ,
which passeth knowledge,
that ye might be filled with
all the fulness of God.
EPHESIANS 3:18–19 KJV

Patty drew her comforter, a white-sale special, up over her sheets and quickly plopped the sham-encased pillows on top of the quilt as the clamor from the twins reached decibels she could no longer ignore. "At least I got the bed made before you two take over my day," Patty told the twins as she lay the damp babies on her bed and began to change their diapers. Coos and gurgles replaced the wails.

"You have no idea how you've changed my life." She gave Jimmy's bottom a pat and turned him over on his stomach before she unfastened Jeanette's diaper. As Jimmy began to fuss and wind up for a loud protest, she hurried the task and scooped up the hungry babies before they began wailing again. She positioned pillows and sat on the bed to nurse Jimmy while she dangled a toy above Jeanette's head to keep her content for a few minutes.

"Two years ago this very month," Patty told her babies, "your mother was standing in the Palazza Davanzati in Florence, Italy, looking at a famous linen bedspread instead of sitting on this white-sale special." She threw her head back in a laugh that made Jimmy startle and pull away. "Sorry." She helped Jimmy get started again. "I was thinking that I doubt if any mother changed diapers or nursed her babies on that gorgeous white coverlet of fancy trapunto work, or it wouldn't be in condition to display its famous scenes of the legendary knight, Tristram."

She giggled, remembering her professor saying how important the bed was considered in the fourteenth century when the quilt was made. "That's for sure. Life begins and ends on a bed."

The doorbell rang. "Are the troops home?" Patty's sister, Karen, called.

"The door's unlocked. Come on in," Patty yelled. "We're back in the bedroom." She patted the mattress. "Sit down. The ladies of the fourteenth century have nothing over me. They entertained their guests on the bed. Of course, the bed covering was a lot fancier than my catalog special." She laughed again. "I was just thinking about the piece of ancient quilt I saw when I was in Italy. Spare me intricately stuffed figures of knights and ladies or leaves and vines for these darlings to spit up on. I'll take a good white-sale quilt any day."

"Maybe after the babies are weaned and potty trained, you can finish the trapunto piece you started, but hang it on the wall," Karen added. "Don't get it near your bed until the twins are eighteen."

"I've probably forgotten how to tug the cord between the row of stitches to puff up the pattern. Can't you just see little fingers messing with the hole in the backing and pulling out the stuffing from the design?"

"Finish it for me," Karen suggested. "I like the extra dimension of the stuffing in a trapunto quilt."

"I've got all the extra dimension I need right now." Patty

pushed her hand against her tummy, still flabby from carrying twins. "These babies stuff the design of my life as pretty as any trapunto quilt and a whole lot fuller."

She gave Jimmy a jounce on the bed and deftly slipped a diaper under his face just before he spit up.

Trapunto quilting is usually done on a solid cover top and backed with a loose woven material that will part easily for the artisan to make a small opening for inserting stuffing or cord to give the picture a three-dimensional appearance. God stuffs our lives full of blessings if we have the eyes to see and recognize them—a healthy appetite, the abundance of food, the love of small children, the affection of a pet. Every day, God inserts cording between the stitched lines of our lives to give us extra dimension. We never fully comprehend the depth and scope of God's love for us and His goodness to us.

GOD'S PATTERN

Practice seeing the hand of God
and being thankful for the blessings
He stuffs into our lives.
He enhances the quality of our days
more than we realize.

A FABRIC PROTEST

Dearly beloved,
I beseech you as strangers and pilgrims,
abstain from fleshly lusts,
which war against the soul.
1 PETER 2:11 KJV

D o you think we can finish the Drunkard's Path quilt in time to make the Temperance Tree before the Ohio State Fair?" Charity asked, pulling her needle through the blue and white quilt.

"We'd better." Birdie blinked. "I don't know how much longer my old eyes can stand this meandering pattern. It makes me dizzy."

"I agree. In my opinion, the organized triangles in the Temperance Tree are more restful," Camille said. "But I think both quilts will sell at the fair, and we'll make good money to contribute to the Women's Christian Temperance Union."

"After we finish these, I propose we make a quilt for the poor Thomas family who live near the creek—might make a few clothes for the children, too. I declare, the family wears nothing but rags." Birdie shook her head.

"It's liquor. Poor Sally works herself to death taking in laundry, but he drinks up every cent she makes and stays too inebriated to make any money himself. Shame. It's time we got Prohibition passed," Faith said.

"I'm glad Frances Willard stepped into the presidency of the Temperance Union. With her organization, women are a force for men to reckon with. About time we stood up and protected our American homes." Everyone nodded in agreement with Birdie.

"I wish I'd been old enough to go with Mother when the women first marched on our Washington Courthouse saloons here in Ohio." Charity smiled at the thought.

"I went," Birdie said. "When we pushed our way inside the taverns and prayed, men ran out of the bars like rats out of a sinking ship. Mother still chortles over closing down eleven taverns in eight days." The women laughed.

"Some of our money needs to go to promoting child labor laws. Take those Thomas children. Those young ones are little tykes for the long hours they work, but the family would starve if they didn't bring home their pittance."

"That's why I spend so much time making quilts and banners. I want to persuade women to join our cause." Faith whacked a loose thread with her scissors. "Society needs change if we want safe homes for women and children."

Many women joined the Women's Christian Temperance Union after the organization began in 1874, motivated by a desire to improve home life and the lot of women. What began as an effort to ban alcohol use expanded to include drug use. Women protested the customary long workweeks of their day and fought for child labor laws and protection against poverty and abuse. Working women's need for child care became a cause and led to a drive to begin kindergartens. Women quilted and made banners calling attention to their causes and rallied others around them. They often used the Union colors of blue and white in their work.

When Frances Willard became the second president of the group, the combination of her organizational skills and charismatic ability to rally support thrust the Woman's Christian Temperance Union into a national force. She rallied women around the well-established relationship of sewing to nurture a family. Women constructed many quilts for the cause. Ironically, Frances herself hated sewing, only making one sampler in her lifetime.

Today alcohol still wrecks families. The MADD organization (Mothers Against Drunk Driving) is another group that began as the outpouring of a mother grieving the death of her child because of a drunk driver. We can be intemperate in many ways, such as our drive for money, our pursuit of recreation, and our conversation. Galatians 5:23 (KJV) gives us a standard, "Meekness, temperance: against such there is no law." The message of the Temperance Tree quilt is as needed today as it was in the 1800s.

$\backsim$

GOD'S PATTERN
God's Word exhorts us to use
moderation in every aspect of our lives.

DIVIDE TO CONQUER

And I saw as it were a sea of glass mingled with fire:
and them that had gotten the victory over the beast,
and over his image, and over his mark,
and over the number of his name,
stand on the sea of glass, having the harps of God.
REVELATION 15:2 KJV

"Your quilt is beautiful." Cindy looked at the spread on her friend's bed. "Did you make it yourself? How long did it take?"

"It took me a year, but I did some other projects at the same time," Kacy answered.

"Didn't you feel discouraged and want to quit? I started a quilt once—shouldn't have tried a full-size quilt. It's too big." Cindy stretched her arms as wide as she could. "I got discouraged and packed it away in the attic. Seeing yours makes me think about getting it out to try again."

"Why don't you? I'll help you. Were you having trouble cutting uniform pieces or what?"

"What I did looked fine, but I felt overwhelmed by how big the whole project was. After working on it for months, there was still so much left to do." Cindy grimaced as she remembered.

"You need to use the divide and conquer principle."

"What's that?"

"You divide your project up into manageable goals. In school when a term paper overwhelmed me, I learned to divide it into chapters and consider only one chapter at a time. The prospect of writing eight pages seems possible. When chapter one was finished, I'd reward myself some way. Then I'd concentrate on chapter two alone. When I realized I had written half the chapters, the rest seemed like an amount I could handle. I still use the divide and conquer plan today for anything I don't want to do or I feel discouraged about completing.

"When I clean house," Kacy continued, waving her hand around the room, "I tell myself I can stop for a reward after I finish each room. Sometimes I stop for a phone call or read one chapter in a novel or walk around the yard. Or I'll promise myself I'll stop after the upstairs and clean the downstairs another day. Once I talk myself into starting and sticking with the job, I often go right through until I finish after all."

Seeing Cindy was interested, Kacy went on pointing to her quilt. "My quilt is divided into fifteen large blocks. I didn't let myself think about how many blocks I needed to make. I'd concentrate on one at a time and reward myself for each finished block. When I reached one-fourth and again when I reached one-third, I'd congratulate myself. By the time I reached halfway or three-fourths finished, I was convinced I could finish. I played a game to force my brain to believe each job was manageable."

Kacy's technique is a valid way to approach an overwhelming or unpleasant task. Revelation 15:2 gives four steps the people needed for victory. First they overcame the beast, then his image, his mark, and finally the number of his names. After conquering this progression, the victor stands on the sea of glass with the harps of God.

If we ask God for His help with tasks, He will unfold a method for us to overcome our obstacles. "O sing unto the LORD a new song; for he hath done marvellous things: his right hand, and his holy arm, hath gotten him the victory" (Psalm 98:1 KJV).

GOD'S PATTERN
Divide difficult challenges into steps
to overcome our endeavors piecemeal.

BUSY HANDS

*A man shall be satisfied with good
by the fruit of his mouth:
and the recompense of a man's hands
shall be rendered unto him.*
PROVERBS 12:14 KJV

*He watereth the hills from his chambers:
the earth is satisfied with the fruit of thy works.*
PSALM 104:13 KJV

My life's a failure, I'm a washed-up has-been." Gail let her teacup clatter against the saucer when she set it down. "Even my kids don't make time for me. I feel useless."

Sarah leaned across the kitchen table and patted Gail's hand before picking up her cup to refill it.

"I hate to admit it but I'm bored with life." Gail lowered her eyes. "Now that my children are grown, nothing breaks the monotony of the days."

"You need a good hobby." Sarah passed the sugar bowl.

"I tried joining a bridge club, but one afternoon was enough for me. The criticism left me bleeding. I bought a kids' oil painting set, but my art would have shamed any self-respecting kindergarten student. My greatest skill is napping, but it's not a hobby destined to enhance self-esteem."

Sarah giggled, and a smile played around the edges of Gail's mouth in spite of herself.

"Don't laugh. You'll spoil my pity party. Hard to feel sorry for yourself and laugh at the same time."

Sarah hugged her friend. "You aren't useless. Your sense of humor rescues many a bleak day for me." She snapped her fingers. "I know the answer. Learn to quilt."

"Quilt! I'd end up with a bag of mismatched fabric scraps to stuff next to my abandoned stick figures in oil paint."

"I'm serious. You'll love quilting. Something about creating useful, pretty quilts brings a lot of satisfaction. Everybody feels loved when I give them a homemade quilt."

"Oh, sure, I'd probably take ten years to make one. One present every decade is not exactly going to flood society with gratitude."

"Give it a try. If you flop, you'll have a great prop for a stand-up comic routine."

To her surprise, Gail enjoyed quilting. She began with a simple Rail Fence pattern and gave it to an elderly woman who was moving into a retirement home. Knowing the gift represented her own handiwork, Gail found a satisfaction and sense of fulfillment from her gift she'd never experienced before.

A handmade quilt represents the investment of one's time and personality that brings an emotional reward. God understands the need we have for a sense of accomplishment. In the Garden of Eden, God set Adam and Eve to "dress and to keep" the garden (Genesis 2:15 KJV). He rewards us with emotional peace when we find productive, useful work to attend. Every phase of life offers opportunities for productivity. When we move from one phase of life to another, we may miss the satisfaction accompanied by the previous stage; but if we ask God, He will show us which profitable activity will fulfill His future plans for us.

GOD'S PATTERN

God designed us to find happiness and joy in productivity.

CUTTING

He that backbiteth not with his tongue,
nor doeth evil to his neighbour,
nor taketh up a reproach against his neighbour.
PSALM 15:3 KJV

Jillian loved Tuesdays. At the craft classes offered on Tuesdays, by the community center near her apartment she discovered a creative knack she never knew she possessed. As much as she enjoyed learning different skills, the women's companionship supplied the most important aspect of the evenings.

"Won't this hot pink sweatshirt look great for the slash quilting we are doing tonight?" Jillian held her shirt up to her chest. "I found a great bargain on sweatshirts."

"Mine's orange. I brought some calico scraps for the heart we are going to sew on the shirts if anyone needs material." Andrea dumped the contents of a plastic bag onto the long table.

"Thanks." Lena took a blue print from Andrea's pile. "This will look good with my red shirt."

After the instructor, Miriam, gave them directions, the women broke into groups to share the center's sewing machines.

"Why would Andrea use a gaudy pink print material on her orange shirt?" Jillian whispered to Lena. "It clashes something awful."

"Her taste in color is tacky." Lena's whisper was louder than Jillian's normal tone of voice. "Her taste in men isn't any better."

"True. She should ditch Dylan. He'll break her heart sure

as I'm standing here." Jillian pinned her calico heart-shaped material behind the front of her sweatshirt.

Andrea's arm reached from behind Jillian and snatched the pink printed cloth Lena held in her hand. "I don't give material to trash who talk about people." Andrea flounced back to the machine behind Jillian's.

Lena gave a grunt of disgust, turned away, and asked Jillian, "May I cut my heart out of your blue stuff?"

Jillian had the grace to flush and without a word handed the fabric to Lena.

The groups of women chattered to the hum of sewing machines while the women sewed their heart-shaped pieces of fabric to the back of their sweatshirts and made rows of stitching, forming diamonds across the heart.

"Everybody has scissors?" Miriam demonstrated how they should cut across each diamond in the shape of an X. "Wash the shirt when you get home, and the sweatshirt material will curl up, exposing the printed fabric behind it and creating the pretty effect of slash quilting. Be careful to cut only the sweatshirt. Don't go too deep with your scissors, or you'll cut the printed material and spoil your work."

The words were hardly out of the instructor's mouth when Jillian groaned. "Oh no! I did what you said not to do. I slashed the calico."

"Let's see if we can patch it." Miriam helped Jillian cut out a new diamond shape, trim away the spoiled material, and stitch the new piece over the mistake. "Well, it's not as good as new, but you'll get enjoyment from your shirt. These raw edges will wear out sooner than if you hadn't slashed too far."

Jillian wasn't thinking about the longevity of her shirt. All she could think about was how her tongue had slashed Andrea. She turned to Andrea behind her. "I'm so sorry I hurt your feelings. I know apologizing really can't fix the hurt, but I enjoy our friendship here at crafts so much, and it bothers me to think I spoiled it with my cutting words."

Our conversation contains the power to slash deeply. The Bible warns us to avoid using our tongue to harm others. The NIV version of Psalm 15:3 says: "And has no slander on his tongue, who does his neighbor no wrong and casts no slur on his fellowman."

GOD'S PATTERN

Take care to speak words that build others up
and avoid those that cut them down.

BARGAIN HUNTING

*"If someone forces you to go one mile,
go with him two miles."*
MATTHEW 5:41 NIV

Look what I found." Jody held up a pieced Puss in the Corner quilt top.

Her friend, Colleen, left the book table in the front yard of the garage sale to join Jody. "Someone went to a lot of trouble to make this. Wonder why they didn't finish it? All it needs is batting, backing, and quilting."

"Isn't it pretty?" Jody looked at the tag pinned to the corner. "The price is a bargain. Do you think our quilt guild would enjoy finishing it?"

"Sure, let's buy it."

The guild enjoyed the striking combination of bold colors. While they quilted, the conversation kept returning to speculation about who pieced the top.

"No one in the family holding the garage sale made it. I asked when I paid for it," Jody said. "No one knew who made it."

"An unsolved mystery. Don't tell me you can resist trying to find out," Colleen challenged her friend.

"The thought had occurred to me," Jody admitted.

A few days later she took the finished piece and returned to the house where she had purchased the quilt top. The lady of the house thought she remembered a neighbor three doors down contributing the piece to the sale. A knock on that door sent her to another nearby home. After talking to a man there,

Jody's search took on a wider range.

She hopped into her car and continued to follow clues until she finally drove up to a one-story brick house. Her heart sank when she saw uncut grass nearly obscuring the sidewalk and several newspapers at the end of the driveway. A cat stood on the front porch and stretched. *Might as well check it out.* Jody climbed out of the car and walked up to the front door.

She knocked. After what seemed a reasonable wait, she started down the steps and heard the door open behind her. There stood a stooped man with bloodshot eyes who needed a shave.

When Jody began her explanation of why she had come and held the quilt out toward him, he straightened and practically ran down he steps.

"That looks like the last quilt my wife made." He reached out to finger it. "But it can't be. She never finished it. She got cancer, and the treatment never helped. It sapped her strength so much she couldn't do anything."

"Maybe it's hers." Jody hoped it was. "My quilt guild finished it because we thought it was pretty, but it wasn't quilted when I bought it at a garage sale. However, the sale was several miles away from here." Her voice dropped as she began to doubt it could be his wife's. "Look, here in the corner," she said, remembering the initials the guild had discovered. "What were your wife's initials?"

"J. B. Her name was Janeene Bower." His eyes grew large as he looked at the initals on the corner. "J. B. It *is* her quilt." Mr. Bower pulled it out of Jody's hands and into his arms. "She's been gone six months. I still miss her. Gave this away because looking at it made me ache inside. It looks like she wanted it to now, all finished and pretty." He ran a finger around the pattern. "May I buy it from you? I think, now, I'd like a reminder of Janeene. It makes me think of her curled up beside me in front of the TV in the evening, holding a quilting hoop and stitching away." Mr. Bower rubbed his sleeve over his eyes.

"I can't seem to get back to normal since she's gone. Guess you can tell by looking at the grass. I'd invite you in, but it's a mess in there, too. Tell you what, come back next Saturday and bring your sewing girls. We'll have a cup of tea, and I'll show you pictures of my Janeene. Prettiest girl in high school."

His eyes took on a pleading look. "Please come back so I can thank everyone. I'll have the lawn cut by then. I'd say that's a good reason to oil the lawnmower and get it going."

"We'll come, Mr.—um, Mr. Bower. You don't need to buy the quilt. It's yours. Would two o'clock be a good time to come?"

"Anytime is good when you're all alone."

Jody retreated to the car before the tears pressing against her eyes watered her cheeks.

Mr. Bower's life turned around as a result of his contact with the quilting women. After a time, Jody told him about her God and how she believed He arranged their meeting to bring comfort. Jody went the extra mile when she undertook the detective work to find the quilt's maker. As a result, an old man found Jesus and some zest for living.

GOD'S PATTERN
God's plan asks us to give more
than is expected.
He multiplies what we give
in unanticipated ways.

THE CACTUS BLOOM

*The wilderness and the solitary place
shall be glad for them;
and the desert shall rejoice,
and blossom as the rose.*
ISAIAH 35:1 KJV

"Everything is brown, beige, or gray if you count the constant cloud cover. What I'd give for a splash of color." Kate stood in the door of her adobe shanty surveying their Arizona surroundings. "Even our home is the color of the earth."

Jerome put his arm around his wife's waist and walked her to the corner of their tiny shelter. "Look at the green in the grove of trees to the south of us." He turned her to their left. "There's green in the grasses in the west."

"Weeds! It's pathetic when we begin to rejoice about weeds." Kate saw the disappointment in his eyes. "All right, so there's some green. Where are the reds and yellows?"

"We'll have the bright color of copper when I begin digging. I'm sure our land is rich with ore."

"I know. We have a blue sky and in the spring, pretty wild-flowers; but I miss the beautiful paintings we could see when we visited the capitol building back home in Richmond, the rainbow of women's dresses when they walked down the street to market or gathered for church services. Virginia is lush with forests, flowers, art, and people. I guess it's really the people I miss the most. As far as our eye can see there's no one but us."

"There's plenty of cattle," Jim began to tease but stopped

when he felt her tense under his arm. "Sweetheart, I know living in Arizona territory is a sacrifice for a city girl, but this is our big chance to own land. Can't you try to find beauty in it?"

Kate leaned back against Jerome's chest. "Well, I guess the cactus has a sort of beauty even if it's not exactly cuddly. I know I'm exaggerating, but my mood is dull, dingy, and lifeless and the land seems to echo it."

"I'll take you to town when I go for supplies next week. I think your egg money should go for the brightest colored material you can find for a new dress."

"You're sweet, but what do I need with a fancy dress out here in the middle of nowhere?"

However, the first thing Kate looked for in the general store in Prescott was fabric.

"Kate!" Nan McCoy stepped through the curtain that partitioned the living quarters from the store. "I thought I heard your voice. It's so good to see you. Come on back and have a cup of tea and a good chat while the men settle their business." Nan held the curtain aside for Kate to enter.

Kate walked straight over to Nan's quilt frame set up in a corner where splashes of red and yellow cloth were pieced into a basket and flower pattern and ready for quilting.

"How beautiful. What's this pattern called?"

"Cactus Bloom. Lots of women here in this desertlike territory are making it because it's so colorful and reminds us of the cactus around these parts."

Kate touched the red. "Jerome said I could buy material for a dress, but I'm going to buy material to make a Cactus Bloom quilt instead. A bright quilt will brighten up our brown surroundings better than anything. I might make a pillow cover also to carry the color around my room."

Kate bought the brightest yellow, red, and green fabric in the general store. Nan tucked in a pattern for the Cactus

Bloom design, drawn on the back of some brown wrapping paper from the store. She wrote instructions for putting the pieces together.

Jerome smiled when he heard the lilt in Kate's voice as they drove their wagon over the sandy soil and barren landscape toward their home.

"Did you good to get into town."

"I'm going to make a beautiful quilt and bring lots of color into our house. Nan McCoy made one, and it's beautiful." Kate bounced on the wagon board in her enthusiasm.

Jerome smiled. "Don't you think this rough road jostles us enough without you jiggling like a schoolgirl?" he teased.

"I'm sorry I complained. If you look around you with an eye to see it, God made lots of beauty in Arizona. As soon as the spring wildflowers come out, I'll sketch some and see if I can design another pretty quilt pattern. That way I'll keep a bit of the summer beauty for us to enjoy in the drab winter." Kate patted her husband's arm. "The quilt will help me remember to thank God for the loveliness of His creation."

Jerome tucked the horse's reins between his knees and turned to give his wife a hug. "With God's help, we'll make this desert bloom," he said.

Although scanty finances and meager resources required frugality and prevented frivolous beauty for beauty's sake, quilts served utilitarian uses as well as provided color and beauty to frontier women's lives. Often made from leftover material, quilts didn't require extra expense.

When our lives seem barren like the desert, God will cause a rose to bloom for us. If we train our eyes to recognize the flower in our wilderness, we'll find reasons to rejoice.

GOD'S PATTERN
He fills our world with physical beauty
to bless our souls regardless
of our circumstances.
His presence in our lives fills our situations
with His beauty when all else is stark and arid.

LAID BACK

But the LORD is in his holy temple:
let all the earth keep silence before him.
HABAKKUK 2:20 KJV

Nicole tapped her toe and threw a magazine onto the windowsill. She'd read every magazine in the coronary unit's waiting room; rather, she had tried to read them. Nothing held her attention more than a few paragraphs. She stood up and stared out the window to the hospital parking lot one story below and wondered briefly what heartache hid in the cars streaming in and out. Did the drivers have a loved one lying in one of the hospital beds hovering between life and death like her husband? Without realizing what she did, she began to pace between the window and the door to the hall. At the end of the hall the nurses bustled in and out of their station. She walked down to see if they had an update on Gordon. They didn't.

"Mrs. Porter, how is your husband?"

Nicole looked around to see Dr. Prescott, the woman who had been on duty when Gordon's ambulance screeched into the emergency room five days ago. Was it only five days? It seemed like three weeks. How the time dragged. What was the date today? She couldn't think.

"It's still nip and tuck," Nicole told the woman. "The cardiologist won't commit to a prognosis."

"How are you coping with the stress?" Dr. Prescott put a sympathetic hand on her arm.

"By fidgeting, I guess." Nicole twisted her hands together.

"What do you do with stress in a situation like this?"

"I quilt." Dr. Prescott gestured toward the tote she carried.

"Quilt? I wouldn't be able to concentrate on sewing. I can't even read a magazine article."

"The emergency room is the scene of a lot of tension. When I first started twelve-hour shifts there, I thought I'd either go bonkers from the pressure of making the right split-second decisions or I'd go mad from boredom when nothing happened for hours on end. Now I quilt between patients. It doesn't require much concentration, and it relaxes me. Tell you what I'll do. I keep a kit on hand ready to begin, pieces cut, and thread and needles assembled. I'll bring a simple one to you tomorrow and show you how to get started."

Dr. Prescott walked away before Nicole could protest.

The quilt the doctor arrived with in the morning was small and looked simple. It involved appliquéing six sunbonnet girls on muslin separated by strips of multicolored material that carried all the colors of the girls' dresses. Their location was already marked on the background fabric.

Reluctant to hurt Dr. Prescott's feelings by rejecting her kind gift, Nicole accepted the quilt and the instructions about how to begin. By noon, she had been allowed in to see her husband twice, and she had stitched down the hats and dresses of two of the girls. She didn't roam between the door and window, and she chattered about the project to her husband, describing the dolls in detail. She thought her husband's eyes showed interest. She traced his lips with one fingertip. Wasn't that a tiny smile?

Before the week was over, Nicole had finished the appliqué. Following Dr. Prescott's directions, she basted the front to the batting and the backing. She enjoyed quilting around the outline of the girls. By the time she had finished the top half of the quilt, she succeeded in making her stitches smaller and smaller and felt pleased with herself. A peace settled over her as she worked on her project. Dr. Prescott was right. Quilting soothed her. By the time Gordon had recovered enough to transfer to another hospital for physical therapy, she had finished the wall hanging. She went to the quilt shop and bought supplies and instructions to begin another one to occupy her time during the long waits for doctors and therapy.

When circumstances agitate us, we can go to God and ask Him to help us become still before Him. By becoming quiet before God, we hear Him better because our agitated and distracted mind gets out of the way. Once we convince ourselves God is not surprised by our situation, we can move on to realizing He is still in control, and we will gain peace. "Be still, and know that I am God" (Psalm 46:10 KJV).

GOD'S PATTERN
God desires for us to
still our minds and thoughts
by realizing He is more powerful
than any of our problems.
When we grow still before Him
we obtain peace.

NEVER SAY NEVER

*To those who by persistence in doing good
seek glory, honor and immortality,
he will give eternal life.*
ROMANS 2:7 NIV

*That ye be not slothful,
but followers of them who through
faith and patience inherit the promises.*
HEBREWS 6:12 KJV

"Are you still working on the same quilt?" Kayla asked her aunt. "You always sew the same blanket every time you come to see us."

"Sure am. Sure do; and I plan to keep on until I finish it." Aunt Eleanor kept her needle working.

"When did you start making those pretty circles? Was I born yet?" Kayla leaned against her aunt's leg.

"I started my Cathedral Window quilt the year you were born."

"Aunt Eleanor, I'm already eight. If you've been making all those little circles for eight years, maybe you'll go to heaven before you finish."

Aunt Eleanor threw her head back in a big laugh then put her quilt down and drew Kayla up on her lap. "Maybe I'll have it finished in time for your wedding."

"I'm going to marry Daddy. Won't he be tired of seeing the quilt?"

Aunt Eleanor gave her another squeeze. "I have to work for my bread and butter since your uncle Rupert died, and I don't have oodles of quilting time. Let me show you why it takes me so long to make one of these little windows." She showed Kayla how the little squares were stitched together and folded back with a piece of colorful material tucked into them.

"It's pretty. Are you really going to give it to me?"

"You can count on it, sweetie pie."

Kayla put her arms around her auntie's neck.

Aunt Eleanor finally did finish the Cathedral Window quilt. Because of the complicated steps required, it took her ten years to make. Years later, she learned a way to make a Cathedral Window quilt much faster on the sewing machine. However, the handmade one always seemed special to her. She said that every time she folded the muslin edges under and stitched them to the pretty calico underneath, forming the oval window, she thought of how God worked in her life. The folds of her life were her trials, but when she turned them over to God and let Him stitch them down, a pretty quality emerged in her character.

GOD'S PATTERN

God knows how to fold the fabric of our lives to expose
lovely qualities and blessings we didn't suspect were there.
He reveals beautiful patterns when we allow Him to trim us.

MISSING HOME

I don't know what to do about Juan. He cries all day long. Poor little guy, I know he's homesick." Allison flipped Juan's chart open on the nurse's desk. "It looks like the antibiotic is working at last, and the infection in his lungs is clearing."

Jolene leaned over Allison's shoulder to check the chart. "He still frets about the traction. He's fidgeted so much he's pulling off parts of the dressings from his leg. He has another surgery in two weeks and then six more weeks of traction."

"I wish his mother could afford to fly in from Guatemala. Nothing like a mama's love."

"She wouldn't have anyone to leave the other children with even if she had the money for a plane ticket. At least you speak Spanish and can communicate with the boy," Jolene said.

The phone rang. "The receptionist said the quilt league is here with the quilts they made for the ward," Allison said when she hung up.

In a few minutes a group of ladies entered wearing bright smiles and carrying armloads of quilts. They passed from bed to bed handing out the quilts. Ruthy was in her wheelchair and received the first one. She threw the white cotton hospital blanket to the floor and wrapped the balloon-covered quilt around her thin legs.

Juan smiled when a lady gave him a quilt with airplanes

stitched all over the front. After the ladies chatted with each patient and tied a balloon to every bed, they left, and the ward became quiet again with many of the children falling asleep from the excitement. Not Juan. When Allison took him his medicine, she found him propped up examining the back of his quilt. "Let's see, Juan, what picture is on your quilt?" She started to turn it over, but Juan stopped her.

"No! See!" he told her in his language. "Look. Here is my country." The material used for the backing of Juan's quilt was a large map. Juan pointed to Guatemala on it and traced his finger around its outline. "This is my home. I'm going back there as soon as my legs are straight. My family will smile when they see me walk."

Allison hugged Juan and continued staring at the quilt. Of all the material the ladies could have used, this fabric showed a map that included Guatemala. Of all the children who could have received the quilt, Juan who lived in Guatemala did. "It's too much for a coincidence," she said. "Thank You, Lord, for blessing a lonely, sick boy." Allison laid her hand on Juan's arm and whispered in Spanish what God had provided for him.

When we know Jesus, our home becomes heaven, the place where we belong. Until then, we live on earth as a visitor, strangers to worldly values. Regardless of where we travel, we are not strangers to people who love God. The brotherhood of believers transcends cultural and geographic barriers. We stand ready to offer hospitality and help fellow Christians, regardless of nationality.

GOD'S PATTERN

Lovers of God offer love and acceptance to Christians of any color, race, or culture. "Now therefore ye are no more strangers and foreigners, but fellowcitizens with the saints, and of the household of God."
EPHESIANS 2:19 KJV

SEIZE THE MOMENT

For he says,
"In the time of my favor I heard you,
and in the day of salvation I helped you."
I tell you, now is the time of God's favor,
now is the day of salvation.
2 CORINTHIANS 6:2 NIV

"Please, let me make this top into a quilt right away. It's the prettiest one I've ever pieced." Edna bit off her blue thread and proudly held up her finished Tennessee Star quilt top.

Mother smiled in admiration. "You did a beautiful job, but you know you have to wait until you are married to do the quilting on any of the tops you've made. Did you start carding the wool from the spring sheep shearing?"

"Not yet. Maybe I'll start tomorrow. Explain to me why I can't quilt. I don't understand why. I have time to quilt now. After I'm married, I'll be busier than ever making shirts for my husband. Then babies will come along. If Bonnie and Melody are any example, I'll be too busy hemming diapers and stitching clothes to quilt my pretty tops."

"Tennessee girls don't quilt until they are married. That's the custom, and we follow custom in this family. I think traditions have their roots in good reasons." Mother stirred the fire in the fireplace before swinging the iron pot on its wrought iron support over the fire. "Stop changing the subject on me. You must begin the wool carding, Edna. Other chores are clamoring for attention. The garden needs hoeing, and soon we'll have crops to sow. I don't want you to develop the habit of procrastination."

"Procrastination! That's exactly what I'm talking about. Why is it I can't put off wool carding, but I can put off quilting and finishing my quilts? Quilt tops are of no use as a single layer of thin cloth. They need to be quilted together with their padding and backing before they supply warmth."

"I've already told you. You have to wait."

"Bonnie and Melody waited, and they've been married for years, but they haven't finished half their tops. If they hadn't received gifts and inherited Grandmother's quilts, they'd freeze in the winters."

"Get to carding, daughter." Mother sent a playful swat in the direction of Edna's backside.

Edna picked up the two wooden paddles with hundreds of thick wires and began to rub wads of wool between the prongs. Each stroke softened the fibers and readied them for spinning into thread later.

Mother took the Tennessee Star top and wrapped it in an old sheet. She lifted the lid of the chest to store it with the others when she spotted another quilt top. Pulling it out she said, "This is a top your grandmother made before she married. She never quilted it afterward. Guess I arrived on the scene and kept her hopping. Would you want to quilt it now? We'll put it in your hope chest when it's done. It'll make a nice remembrance of your granny."

"I'd love to finish Granny's quilt. It'll help me practice tiny stitches." She winked at Mother. "I'll never tell you let me quilt before I was married."

Many quilt tops are put together but never quilted. The enthusiasm of creation often dissipates if put aside for a time instead of continuing until completed. The same principle holds true of spiritual hunger. If the spiritual cravings of our soul are not fed, the desire to learn and grow spiritually may atrophy. One should never delay learning spiritual principles and putting them into practice. Nor do we want to procrastinate telling others about salvation. Now is the day to receive Jesus and to develop a personal relationship with Him.

GOD'S PATTERN

God's Word encourages us to persevere
for a close relationship with God.
"However, I consider my life worth nothing to me,
if only I may finish the race and
complete the task the Lord Jesus has given me—
the task of testifying to the gospel of God's grace."
ACTS 20:24 NIV

THE WEDDING GIFT

I wonder if your grandmother will feel well enough to attend your wedding." Faye set a bag of groceries on the kitchen table where her daughter, Hayley, sat writing thank-you notes for early wedding gifts. "I stopped by there on the way to the store. She admitted her arthritis is acting up worse than ever."

Hayley put down her pen. "She told me the same thing when I phoned her. She said her hands hurt too much to hold a needle, and there was no way she could finish my wedding quilt." Hayley blinked to keep tears back. "I told her not to feel bad because I understood, but she said she's made a Double Wedding Ring quilt for every grandchild when they married, and she hates fizzling out on the youngest one."

"I was afraid of that, but I agree she can't do it. Sorry, honey, you're the only one not to receive a Grandma quilt. What she isn't admitting is that she can't see to thread a needle, and some of her most recent work really needs to be ripped out. . .it's crooked. Her macular degeneration has ruined her eyesight."

Hayley's blinking wasn't working. "I told her not to worry about it. It doesn't take a quilt for me to know she loves me, but I'm disappointed and can't seem to help crying about it."

"Brides have an extra measure of emotion as the big day approaches. A few tears probably do you good and get rid of the tension of planning a wedding."

Hayley expected the last week before her wedding to spin with activity, but she didn't expect every sister, cousin, and aunt to bustle about as much as she and her mother did.

"Can't someone go to the mall with me this afternoon and help me pick up the bridesmaid gifts?" Hayley asked before her sisters grabbed up their coats and left.

"Sorry, we don't have time." The door banged behind them.

"You'd think they were the bride," Hayley said, grumbling all the way to her car.

Later as they left the wedding rehearsal for the dinner, Hayley worried out loud. "I feel like we are forgetting things. Do you think we're ready?"

"Think so. Our mistress of ceremonies is taking care of meeting the florist at the church tomorrow. We're going to pick up Grandma for the rehearsal dinner tonight. She said a little thing like pain wasn't going to stop her from attending your rehearsal dinner and the wedding."

When only chicken bones were left on the plates, and the last of the key lime pie was devoured, Hayley's father stood to reminisce about his daughter's childhood. "It's time for the surprise," he said as he finished his remarks. Mother wheeled Grandma's wheelchair to the front of the room. She held a large package on her lap. Hayley was glad she was sitting down when she opened her package. There in her lap lay the Double Wedding Ring quilt her grandmother had begun but couldn't finish.

"Grandma, how did you do this? I thought it was impossible."

"It was if I had to do it myself with these old eyes and hands. Your sisters, aunts, and cousins have spent practically every waking moment at my house, working on your quilt. No one wanted you to be the only grandchild to marry without one."

Strong families serve one another. A strong family provides

a sense of security and stability. When help is demanded, it fractures families. When help is volunteered, all parties receive a blessing.

GOD'S PATTERN
Love finds pleasure in serving.

POSSESS THE LAND

Fifty-four Forty or Fight. Fifty-four Forty or Fight," the men chanted as they marched down Main Street of Oregon City in the Oregon northwest. The cadence kept Ralph's feet skipping by his father's side. Ralph waved his sign with vigor. It urged, "DEMOCRAT JAMES K. POLK FOR PRESIDENT." His father's sign read: "SAVE OUR OREGON FROM GREAT BRITAIN'S LAND GRAB." When Ralph passed some classmates on the sidewalk, he puffed out his chest as far as he could to show off the big Polk for President campaign button pinned to his coat.

The men's march to raise awareness of the boundary issue ended at their headquarters. Ralph was first in line for hot coffee to quench his thirst. He grabbed a doughnut, sat down, and bent to untie his shoe to relieve his aching feet before he caught the stern shake of his father's head, who was talking politics.

"Smart of Polk to use the 54°40' latitude line as a campaign slogan for his 1845 presidential run. Hope our march helps keep the heat on the U.S. government to settle the boundary dispute."

"Sure is an important issue here in our Oregon region. I have my eye on some forest land on the forty-ninth parallel, but I'd like to know what country the land south of the 54°40' parallel belongs to before I put up the money."

Ralph wasn't sure what all those numbers meant, but he knew that Douglas fir forests would mean good business for his family.

"Russia gave up her claims south of the 54°40′ parallel. I'm ready to fight for it." Ralph's eyes grew big at the bold words of his father's friend.

For a while longer Ralph tried to follow the men's talk about the controversy with Great Britain over where the northern boundary line of the Oregon region should lie, but soon the hot drink and doughnuts combined with the miles his short legs had walked began to make him drowsy. He put his head on the table where the men had piled their placards and fell sound asleep with the rhythm of Fifty-four Forty or Fight still ringing in his head.

Ralph's mother and her friends raised the awareness of the border dispute by making quilts with what they called the "Or Fight" pattern. The ladies pieced a pattern of squares and triangles that created a pretty star when combined together into a block. They alternated each star block with a plain block. At quilting bees they giggled when they caught themselves joining their sons in chanting "or fight." Children latched onto the chant, enjoying its repetition. Ralph cheered as loudly as anyone when Polk won the election.

"Do you think Polk will make us a territory now that he's president?" Ralph asked his father.

"Someday we'll probably be a state."

Before 1846, when a treaty with Great Britain established the border on the forty-ninth parallel, Ralph and his classmates in Oregon studied more about geography and the lines used to establish locations on maps.

They learned about the imaginary lines of latitude that parallel the equator and are measured in degrees and minutes. Then the students understood better what their catchy jingle meant. When Ralph learned that one degree equaled sixty nautical miles and one minute measured one nautical mile, he realized how much land was at stake between the different parallel lines.

The borders of a country are drawn by politicians, and many wars have been fought over them. But God determined the boundaries of our world. He set the firmament in place and established how far the oceans could come up on the land. God draws boundaries for our personal lives. He knows the right time to enlarge our lives, broaden our understanding, or increase our realm of influence.

GOD'S PATTERN
God's plan is to increase and enlarge
our relationships, our capacity for love, and our skills.
He wants us to possess the land
by taking the gospel message
to others wherever we go.

UNDERSTANDING

And the Word was made flesh,
and dwelt among us.
JOHN 1:14 KJV

Tell me again what you want me to order for my store." Fred Burns looked over the counter at the two avid quilters. "I've already expanded my quilting section to twice its size, and you mean I still don't have everything you want?" He shook his head. "Are you never satisfied?"

"You try your hand at making quilts, and you'll see what we need."

Fred may have imagined it, but he could have sworn he heard a huff as the lady turned and marched out the store door.

"Dare you," the remaining lady said, placing the strap of her purse on her shoulder and starting out.

"Dare me to what?" Fred asked.

"Make a quilt, or would it offend your masculine pride?"

The words rolled around in his head the rest of the day. Many days, he realized, more quilters came to his store for supplies than garment sewers. Any good salesman knew a paramount principle for sales was understanding the needs of his customers. Besides, he resented the underlying implication he was too macho to quilt. He was selling sewing supplies, for goodness' sake. Didn't that show sensitivity to women's needs?

By the time he closed up the store, Fred had pored over the pattern books and decided he could handle the Maryland Beauty pattern. Surely a pattern of only two patches wouldn't present a daunting challenge. Armed with how-to books and a bag of red and blue printed fabric, he headed for home eager to tell his wife about his new project and how it would increase the store's business.

"Can you just see it now? A quilt hanging in the window made by a man, and the manager of the store to boot."

As the months flew by, Fred still wrestled with his quilt, glad he had not told anyone but his wife about the project. Overcoming mistake after mistake, at last Fred finished the top and tackled the quilting. In a short time, he decided his masculine pride would survive if he hired someone else to quilt his comforter. When at last the pretty patchwork hung in the window, women flocked to see the quilt a man had pieced.

He was also right about understanding the needs of his customers. He wasted no time ordering numerous gadgets to help measure, cut, and sew. A new line of lamps and machines soon graced his shelves. Impressed by his increased ability to sympathize with the frustrations and failures of his customers, women brought him their quilting problems. Buoyed by success, Mr. Burns became an enthusiastic maker of quilt tops. He tackled harder and harder patterns and became a valuable resource to quilters who sought his advice and stayed on to buy fabric or supplies while they were there. He experimented with the latest developments in quilt making. But he never learned to like quilting after the top was finished. He always hired the job out, glad to part with the money it cost.

People long for understanding. They want other people to understand their agonies and their aggravations. We also want God to understand the cries of our hearts. Yet fear prompts us to wonder how God can love us if He *does* understand us. God became flesh when Jesus was born on earth, and as a man He identified with every part of the human condition. God's understanding of the inner workings of our minds and souls is complete and full of compassion. He understands our needs; and, best of all, He is fully able to meet them beyond our comprehension.

GOD'S PATTERN

God designed a way mankind could
understand the Godhead when He took on
the form of man at the birth of Jesus.
No patterns of human reactions are
foreign to His knowledge or
beyond His redeeming love.

DECORATING

Them hath he filled with wisdom of heart,
to work all manner of work, of the engraver,
and of the cunning workman, and of the embroiderer,
in blue, and in purple, in scarlet,
and in fine linen, and of the weaver,
even of them that do any work,
and of those that devise cunning work.
EXODUS 35:35 KJV

I called to let you know you have a little longer to finish the wall hanging for the house dedication. Several of the Habitat for Humanity team working on this house are down with the flu. We are too shorthanded to finish the house on time. You wouldn't have time to come help with the finishing touches on the house, would you?" Jackie asked as an afterthought.

"Sorry, I'm a lot better pushing a needle than swinging a hammer," Serita answered. "I'll have the wall hanging ready by dedication. I hope the family isn't too disappointed with the delay."

"They have the flu, too, so they can't help either. We'll all be glad when they can leave their dilapidated apartment for a fresh start in this pretty rancher."

"My quilt has daffodils and butterflies to symbolize new beginnings," Serita said. "It'll look great hanging in the entryway. I hope the family likes it."

"They will. They're hardworking people who really needed a break. Their son, Lorenzo, will love your butterfly symbol.

He can't wait to get the cast off his leg after his latest surgery. We all hope he can begin to walk now. Thanks again for doing the hanging. Tell your quilt guild the next Habitat house is scheduled for a June completion date. We really appreciate the guild supplying beautiful wall hangings. Something lovely to decorate a new home means a lot."

"My sister liked the hanging so much when she visited me this spring, she's persuaded her quilt guild to make quilts for each new house Habitat for Humanity builds in her community," Serita said.

We all enjoy decorating our home as an expression of our personalities. Handmade items make our homes unique to us. God gave directions for elaborate decorations for the tabernacle and, later, the temple when it was built. The finest artisans did the engraving, weaving, and embroidering for the tabernacle furnishings. God understood the need for beauty in the human soul. Our homes are a refuge from the world, its pressures, and confusion. The most important decoration we can provide for our homes is the presence of peace. By visiting the tabernacle, the Israelites found the peace of God. By daily visiting with God in Bible reading and prayer, we bring peace to our souls, which causes an atmosphere of serenity for those living in our home. When we decorate our homes with items that remind us of God, we will encourage our minds to consider God and the peace only He can supply.

GOD'S PATTERN

God encourages us to
use our talents to create beauty for
ourselves and for others.

TEETHING DOG

But as for you, ye thought evil against me;
but God meant it unto good,
to bring to pass, as it is this day,
to save much people alive.
GENESIS 50:20 KJV

Christmas dawned early for the Maguire family. Smuggled into the garage before the first rays of morning light, Lady, a six-week-old German shepherd puppy, refused to sleep in her new bed. Her howling soon had the entire family downstairs, where they all shared Lady's wet kisses and tail-wagging excitement.

Lady bounded around the family room adding noise and confusion to the gift opening. Every whoop of enthusiasm over a gift brought Lady romping to share the thrill.

"Wow, Mom, did you make this for me?" Dan threw the Christmas wrapping paper aside and held up the quilt his mother had made for her son's last Christmas before graduating from high school.

"I made this map of the world on the front to remind you that the world's yours to conquer when you leave school next June," Julie explained. "I made each country using materials left over from the clothes I made you while you were growing up."

"Cool."

Julie smiled at Dan's pleasure. Lady barked her approval, jumped onto Dan's lap, and plopped down on the quilt.

"Down." Dan stood up abruptly, dumping Lady off the

quilt and onto the floor. "No, you don't. Mom put too much work into this for puppy shenanigans."

Lady held different ideas. One day Dan came home from school to find the puppy had used the quilt for a teether. She'd gnawed a large hole where the backing sheet turned to the front to form a border.

"Bad dog!" Dan stamped his foot at Lady. "You can't come in my room again when I'm away." Dan almost slammed the door on Lady's nose.

"Makes me mad, too." Julie scowled at the pup. "I'll try to fix the quilt. I have a piece of sheeting left over to use as a patch over the hole. It won't look as good as new, but it's the best we can do. Are you worth the nuisance you cause?" she asked, grabbing Lady by the collar and taking her outdoors.

She was. After a romp in the yard with a stick, Dan forgave Lady. Although his room and the quilt remained off-limits while she was a puppy, Lady eventually outgrew her penchant for chewing and became a well-behaved and cherished pet.

When she died years later, the scars on the quilt from her puppyhood escapade became a special treasure. Happy memories of Dan's beloved dog surfaced every time he looked at the patch.

We often stand amazed at how God takes occurrences that seem disastrous to us and turns them into blessings. We cannot anticipate the twists an event will take later on in life that bring a different meaning to what we thought was a total calamity.

In the account of Joseph in Genesis, his years of imprisonment for no fault of his own seem a horrible fate and totally unjust. The years he spent in jail could have caused him to nourish bitterness and regret for wasted years. Instead, Joseph used the years in captivity to perfect leadership skills and to listen to the voice of God. These qualities led to his release. God used him to administer policies in Egypt that caused it to prosper in a time of famine and allowed him to gain the favor of Pharaoh. The stored food in Egypt allowed Joseph to give refuge to his family and spare their lives from starvation. God's power to change the disastrous into blessing is no different today. He knows the best route and timing to bring blessing to each of our situations, even if we feel that our circumstances are a terrible waste and highly unjust.

GOD'S PATTERN

God's power is greater than our enemies.
He will bring good out of what appears
to be regrettable if we put our disappointments
into His hands and watch for His mercy.

Here Comes the Groom

Let us be glad and rejoice,
and give honour to him:
for the marriage of the Lamb is come,
and his wife hath made herself ready.
REVELATION 19:7 KJV

How many pieces of fabric have you collected for your Charm quilts?" Wilma asked her two friends as they sat under a tree working on embroidery samplers during school recess. The girls, in their last year of formal schooling, often brought their needlework for recess instead of romping on the school ground like the younger children.

"Not very many. I'll be as old as Methuselah before I collect 999 different pieces of material for a Charm quilt. I don't understand why every piece has to come from a different cloth." Tabitha sucked her finger to stop the bleeding from a needle prick.

"Tabitha, you need to try harder so you won't reach Methuselah's age before you meet your prince charming and get married." Wilma turned her head. "Priscilla, we had better round up some material for Tabitha's Charm quilt and save her from becoming an old maid. Did I give you a swatch from my niece's baby quilt fabric?" Wilma asked.

"You gave me some. It brought me up to 995 pieces." Priscilla waved her embroidery hoop. "Hurrah, I'm almost ready to meet my future husband."

"It's not fair. You've already met him," Tabitha complained. All the girls looked to the field across from the schoolhouse where they could see Seth following a team of horses around and around preparing the land to plant with corn.

Priscilla blushed and ducked her head behind her handwork.

"What's Seth going to give you for your one thousandth piece?"

"Maybe he won't give me anything." Priscilla pretended to look shocked.

"He has to. You know the last piece of the Charm quilt has to come from your intended's garment." Wilma sighed. "You're going to be the first one of us to marry. I only have eighty pieces, and Randy probably hopes I'll take a long time to gather the rest."

"Make Seth give you a chunk of his work shirt. That's something he's been wearing close to his heart," Tabitha suggested.

"Look at our blushing bride," Wilma teased as Priscilla turned an even deeper red.

"Maybe I don't blush good enough. Maybe that's the trouble," Tabitha offered.

"The trouble is you don't have nearly enough different materials to make a Charm quilt. Why do you think it's called a Charm quilt? The charm is your prize, a husband. Priscilla, we have to help Tabitha out with her fabric. The reason I have so much is because my relatives in the East send me scraps from their quilting bees. I'll write them to send you some. Wouldn't do for you to be an old maid." Wilma shook her head.

Tabitha smoothed the escaping strands of her hair back into the bun caught at the nape of her neck with a brown ribbon matching her dress. "I'm not sure I want to make a Charm quilt anyway. I seem to stick myself more than the rest of you do. Then I make a bloody mess out of whatever I'm working on." She sucked her finger again. "Maybe I don't have enough domestic skills to marry. I'd rather ride a horse than sew any day."

"That makes Bret the right husband for you. He has plenty of horses and needs an active wife to help out with his pig farm."

Wilma giggled, and Tabitha stuck her tongue out.

"Smelling like a pig isn't my idea of a charming ending."

A custom in some areas of the country in the middle 1800s was for young, unmarried girls to make Charm quilts. The legend held that when a girl gathered 999 pieces of different fabric, she would meet the man she would marry; and he would give her a piece of material from one of his garments to make the one thousandth piece for her quilt. By focusing on her needlework and preparing a quilt for her new household, the young girl was preparing herself for necessary wifely sewing skills.

The Bible tells us our Lord, Jesus Christ, will return at the Second Coming to claim His bride, the church, and exhorts us to make ourselves ready. Many a quilter might wish 999 swatches of cloth were all they needed, because a peek into their closet would confirm they had already achieved that goal. A better preparation for the coming of our Lord, however, is to trust in Jesus' work on the cross and submit to His influence.

GOD'S PATTERN

To God, the most important trait for us to
acquire is a Christlike character. As we study the Bible,
we see the pattern Jesus set for us to follow.
By asking the Holy Spirit to mold us into His image,
we will gradually collect more and more Christian attributes.

OUT OF SIGHT

Thy word is a lamp unto my feet,
and a light unto my path.
PSALM 119:105 KJV

"Where's the quilt?" Bonnie asked, looking around her neighbor's room. "I thought you invited us to come help quilt your Drunkard's Path top."

"I did, but I waited until you came to get it out." Cora laid out some packets of needles.

"Won't it be hard for lots of us to quilt at the same time if you don't have it on a quilt frame?"

"We'll quilt on a frame," Cora said.

"It takes awhile to get a quilt set up on a frame. That'll subtract from our quilting time."

Cora laughed. "The frame comes down easier if we have two people, one on each rope."

Bonnie lifted her head upward, her eyes following Cora's pointing finger. "You have your quilt frame on the ceiling! I've never seen such a thing."

"Here, put these two ladder-back chairs about a yard apart over by the coffee table, and I'll place these two over here." The women positioned the chairs. "Now, grab that rope behind the window curtain there, and I'll get ahold of this one." Cora reached behind the bookcase. "Let the rope out a little at a time until the frame comes down far enough to rest on the backs of the chairs."

"Well, I'll be." Bonnie stepped over to look at the red

and white quilt top already basted to the batting and backing and rolled up with only a yard of the length exposed, ready for quilting. "It's out of sight when you aren't quilting, and ready to go when you are. What a good idea."

The ladies made so much progress on the quilt during the afternoon that they stopped once, rolling the quilt on the frame to expose another few feet in order to sew farther down the comforter.

Just as Bonnie kept her quilt hidden out of the way but handy for the times she wanted to quilt, we need to keep the word of God hidden in our heart and ready for the unexpected moment when we need it for our guidance, comfort, or counsel. When we memorize verses, the appropriate Scripture will pop into our minds when we need it. By studying the Bible, we become familiar with its wisdom and instruction and store the knowledge in our minds and souls ready for our instant use. Knowledge of God's Word is better than having a wise tutor whispering in our ear.

∽

GOD'S PATTERN

The Word of God lights the way we should go,
preventing us from getting off the narrow path ordained by God.
By memorizing Bible verses,
we adhere better to God's pattern.

STEADY

*And he said, Who art thou, Lord?
And the Lord said,
I am Jesus whom thou persecutest:
it is hard for thee to kick against the pricks.*
ACTS 9:5 KJV

W hat are you doing crawling around on the ground like that, Grandma?" Jason asked.

"I'm basting my quilt top to the batting and the backing." Grandma eased off her knees and straightened up into a sitting position.

"But you're making your pretty top look all ugly with those big black threads crisscrossing it," Jason protested.

"Does make it look a bit unsightly, doesn't it?" Grandma reached out a hand to Jason. "Help me get up. Once my bones get down here, they don't want to rise again."

Jason pulled until Grandma was standing upright.

"Those ugly stitches will hold the quilt still so all the fabric will stay in the right position while I stitch. It may look a mess now, but after I finish the quilting, the comforter will look better because it can't slip while I sew. Jason, give my knees a rest by finishing the basting on this quilt top for me."

"Me! I don't know how."

"It's easy. Make three- or four-inch stitches across every Dresden Plate design, horizontally and then vertically like this." Grandma pointed to the one she had just completed.

"But I don't want to sit around inside. I want to run over

221

to the railroad tracks and see if I can put a penny on the track before a train passes."

Grandma laughed. "You are as bad as the quilt layers. Unless we baste you down, you wiggle away and do something dangerous. You know your dad doesn't want you going to the tracks. Listen to him, and you won't be sorry." Grandma threaded a needle for Jason and was soon snoring in a chair while Jason crawled about basting and fuming. He kicked the floor with impatience. "Ow," he yelped as he stuck his finger.

Grandma jerked awake. "You're just like Paul in the Bible kicking against the pricks. Sometimes these ornery little jobs teach us something important like stick-to-itiveness. Once I made a quilt without taking the time to baste it. In places the batting bunched, making unsightly bumps in the quilt. In other places the backing fabric folded over, making creases instead of a smooth back. Don't try to skip the necessary steps for whatever you want to do in life. You may not understand God's plan for you, but when you cooperate and don't kick against the pricks, His plan prevents lumps and folds in your life. I can finish it now. You run outside but not down to the railroad tracks." Jason rolled his eyes.

The three layers of a quilt require basting to hold them in place before the quilter can move on to the more rewarding work of quilting the layers together. Today some quilters use dozens of safety pins to hold the thicknesses together. Others use the longest setting on the sewing machine and roll the material as they sew to make room for it at the right of the presser foot. Whatever method a quality quilt receives, the boring and unsightly step of basting helps ensure a beautiful finished work. Many times we need to hold still and cooperate with the steps and stages God uses as He works in our lives. God knows what processes will form us into an attractive and practical person best equipped for His purposes. God's steps of preparation enable us to accomplish the goals the Lord has planned for our lives.

GOD'S PATTERN

Even though some of the steps
God uses in our lives
seem boring or unpleasant,
God doesn't skip the processes
that make us into
the lovely person He has planned.

WELL DONE

But covet earnestly the best gifts:
and yet show I unto you a more excellent way.
1 CORINTHIANS 12:31 KJV

Latisha cradled the quilt in her hands. She turned her back on the proprietor of the secondhand store so he couldn't read the excitement in her face. "What a find," she whispered to Sabrina, her companion from the historical society staff. "It's an old sample of English piecing. To think, we almost gave up finding something of historical importance and quit looking."

Latisha turned the honeycomb design of the quilt over and peered at the back. "See. The paper templates are still basted to the medallions. There's writing on the paper, and it looks old. Wonder what secrets the templates will tell us?"

The rows of faded medallions were still pretty, and the colors ranged from muted shades of red to pinks softened by age. Each medallion looked like a flower in a perfect hexagon shape.

"No wonder the pattern is called Flower Garden." Latisha fingered a flower. The paper template behind the material gave each hexagon a crisp, perfect shape, all six sides exactly the same in length. She handled the material with caution in case the paper backing was brittle from age. Each piece of paper held the handwriting of what appeared to be a personal letter before it had been cut into templates.

Still trying to act nonchalant in order not to drive the price up, Latisha turned to the storekeeper and asked, "Are there any more medallions that go with this unfinished Grandmother's Flower Garden quilt?"

"No, ma'am. Just what you see. Don't know why the owner never finished it."

"How much do you want for the unfinished quilt top?" Latisha tried to make her voice sound uninterested.

"Well, it's awfully dusty and old, and there aren't any matching pieces to finish it, so I reckon I'll let it go cheap. Might make a nice wall hanging. Seems strange the quilter sewed the material down to paper."

"The paper pattern makes each hexagon stay true to its form." Latisha whipped out her wallet and handed the man the price he'd asked for the treasure before he could change his mind and raise it.

Back at her office in the historical society, Latisha pulled out a magnifying glass and settled under a bright lamp. The material edges were ironed and tacked over the old paper, making a careful crease so the six sides were exactly the same. The sides were whipped together at the edge using a red medallion at the center of each flower, surrounded by two rows of rose and pinks in shades going from light to deep. Each pretty flower contained nineteen perfect hexagons. The flowers were stitched to a row of black hexagons before the next flower was attached.

However, it was the back that fascinated Latisha and Sabrina. The words "I pledge you my undying love" were easy to read across the middle of one paper template. Some of the words were cut away, but the next line read "In spite of our troubles."

"What do you suppose troubled this quilt maker?" Latisha wondered.

"Look. Here's a date." Sabrina pointed to another template.

"It was 1775. Maybe the woman's beloved had to leave England to fight for the British in the Revolutionary War."

"This piece gives a new slant: 'No matter what Father says,'" Latisha read. "Maybe her father was stifling her romance."

The paper on the next hexagon bore a different handwriting. "'Stir in one egg and a fistful of sugar.' Possibly that was the recipe for the wedding cake," Sabrina offered.

Latisha laughed. "Since her father nixed the whole affair, the poor girl cut up her love letters and her cake recipe for a quilt instead."

"We are a couple of hopeless romantics." Sabrina rolled her eyes at their wild leap into speculation.

"I started a Grandmother's Flower Garden quilt myself years ago. This antique makes me want to get it out and finish it. I ironed my fabric edges over hexagons made of freezer paper, so the quilt will never tell any of my secrets. It's practical and cheap but lacks the fascination of our historical find."

"Why take the time to cut out all those paper pieces?" Sabrina asked.

"I can't imagine making the edges match up perfectly without using the stiff template to iron and tack over. Sharp, perfect edges made matching a cinch. It's an excellent way to do it."

God's ways are excellent. He has ways for us to approach life and its problems that are more excellent than man's ways.

~

GOD'S PATTERN

Seek God for
the most excellent way
to live our lives.

MERCY

For thou, Lord, art good,
and ready to forgive;
and plenteous in mercy unto all
them that call upon thee.
PSALM 86:5 KJV

The three women moved their tongues faster than their needles as Crystal drove them to the quilt show in the state capital. Laughter made the miles pass quickly—too quickly.

"Oh, no," Crystal moaned at the wail of a siren and the blue rotating flash from a police car behind her. "Mercy, Lord, I don't need a ticket. Forgive me."

The nervous women stitched even faster as the policeman approached.

The man strode to Crystal's window with a pad and pen poised to write a ticket. "You were going 65 in a 55-mile-per-hour zone." He leaned down to look at Amber in the front passenger seat. "You quilting, ma'am?" he asked.

"Yes, sir," Amber mumbled, wondering if somehow her activity made the speeding offense worse.

The officer peered into the backseat where the women held their needles as if frozen in mid-stitch. "You're quilting, too? My mother used to quilt. My wife and I sleep under her Flower Basket quilt."

"We're on our way to Richmond to see a quilt show," Crystal managed to say.

"You need to slow down so you'll live to see the show,

ma'am." The patrolman slid his pen into the clipboard clasp and dropped the board to his side.

"Yes, sir." Crystal didn't have to try to sound meek.

"My mother won ribbons at quilt shows," the policeman said. "Quilters are law-abiding people at heart. You folks go along now, but watch your speed. Hope you win a ribbon." He waved them back onto the highway.

"Wow, that was close." Amber let out a pent-up breath. "Can you imagine, a policeman whose mother quilted?"

"It's God's mercy, that's for sure," Crystal said. "I've always heard grace is undeserved mercy," she added.

GOD'S PATTERN

God's mercy is available for
everyone who repents.

TRIED AND TRUE

With the ancient is wisdom;
and in length of days understanding.
JOB 12:12 KJV

L ouise hung up the phone with a bang.

"What's the matter?" Her husband, Bill, looked up from the newspaper.

"That was my sister saying Mom and Dad want us to give them an anniversary party. I don't have time to plan a party with the huge quilt exhibit opening next month."

"It would be a good way to honor your parents. Maybe if I help you, we can manage a celebration."

"But they want to speak to the guests and share their gems of wisdom from life. That could get embarrassing."

"They have learned a lot from life we all could benefit from hearing," Bill said from behind his newspaper.

The possibility of a party kept intruding into Louise's thoughts as she prepared large displays of quilting history to go with the actual quilts for the museum.

Poring over musty library books, she discovered artwork that showed evidence that material was quilted long ago, but the ravages of time destroyed any fabric remnants of the ancient needlework. Pictures of quilted fabric proved the existence of the quilting method. She was fascinated to learn about the oldest existing quilt. Found on the floor of a Scythian chieftain's tomb, in the part of Asia that later became the Soviet Union, the quilt of appliquéd animals is thought to be from the period of 100 B.C. to A.D. 200.

None of the quilts she was preparing for display were as old as the ones she read about. In the Middle Ages, inventories listing household items for tax purposes often mentioned quilts. Agnes de Faucigny, in her will of 1262, left her feather bed and its quilted cover to a convent because she was grateful for the care she received growing up in the nunnery.

As a museum curator, Louise valued old things and appreciated the glimpse they provided into bygone days. Even old newspapers left a record of advertisements advising of classes to teach quilting. Quilted clothes enjoyed popularity in England of the seventeenth and eighteenth centuries. In the 1500s quilting found a place in the bedroom for sleepwear.

But it was her reading about the Saracens of Arabic origin who conquered Spain and Sicily and wore quilted jackets topped by chain mail around A.D. 700 that set her thinking about her parents. Arabic peoples' quilted material was brought to Europe after their invasions, either reviving a skill of long ago or introducing it for the first time. Either way, the Europeans profited from the Saracens' work; and quilted garments became part of life in Europe. The things the Saracens made for their comfort and protection made a difference in lands far away and in years to come.

Louise thought about learning from her parents' wisdom and profiting the easy way from what they had learned the hard way. By valuing their experiences, she could bypass some of her parents' pitfalls. By gleaning their bits of wisdom, she could enrich her own life. Louise now saw the anniversary party as an opportunity for her parents to influence others just as the museum displays informed people of the value of ancient history. Before the day was over, she was on the phone to her sister with plans for skits from her parents' lives and making posters to hang throughout the church hall, containing gems from her parents' mouths.

Established mores of our society are often built on the learned wisdom of man accumulated over the ages. We ignore or fail to learn about the underlying wisdom behind our customs to our own peril. Society is built on patterns we shouldn't ignore. "Remove not the ancient landmark, which thy fathers have set" (Proverbs 22:28 KJV). Contrary to today's society, which tries to persuade us that these landmarks are useless, they were established because they benefit humanity.

GOD'S PATTERN

God has planted wisdom in the lives
and customs of our elders and our society.
Our lives go more smoothly and many trials are
avoided if we listen to the wisdom of
our elders and take care not to ignore
the landmarks of the past.

UGLIEST QUILT CONTEST

LORD, thou hast heard the desire of the humble:
thou wilt prepare their heart,
thou wilt cause thine ear to hear.
PSALM 10:17 KJV

"Don't be ridiculous! No way I'm going to enter the Ugliest Quilt Contest. I'd probably win. Can you think of anything more humiliating?" Monica handed the magazine entry form back to her friend, Chelsea. "If embarrassment is your favorite way to get your kicks, you can enter. Me, I prefer to goof up my quilts anonymously."

"The annual contest is just for fun, Monica—a good chance to laugh at yourself." Chelsea held the form. "I think I *will* enter. I need all the laughs I can get. Besides, the prize money spends as good as any other contest money."

"Yeah, sure, accompanied with national notoriety and public shame—complete with magazine pictures. I don't go in for self-flagellation." Monica picked up her quilt and held it close to Chelsea's face. "Look at my crooked, uneven stitching!" Monica flipped it over to the back. "I caught the backing into tiny pleats over and over. It's bad enough that my quilt group saw this disgraceful quilting at the guild meeting."

Chelsea laughed. "None of us makes perfect quilts. I'm going to enter the one where I appliquéd some of my flower baskets upside down. I don't care if it does end up as a picture in the quilt magazine. If it makes other people feel superior to me, I can count it as my good deed for the month."

Monica folded up her quilt. "I envy your nonchalant outlook on life," she said. "I guess I care too much about what people think."

Chelsea chewed her lower lip. "I didn't feel nonchalant last month when my son was picked up by the police for petty theft." A sob caught in Chelsea's throat. "I cared what people thought. Dealing with George since he started running with a drug-using crowd has been a good lesson in humility. Wish I could say all my mistakes were as inconsequential as quilts."

Monica put her arm around her friend's shoulder. "God is going to hear your cries about George. The Bible says He will draw near to the humble. You showed that attitude to everyone in our church circle when you shared some of the things you thought you'd done wrong raising George. I'll bet you spared a lot of moms the heartache of making the same blunders. After we've messed up, the important thing is to learn from our experience and go on. God forgives when we ask." Monica continued to pat Chelsea on the back.

"Listen to me talk. Since a humble attitude brings God close, I guess it'd be good for me to enter that contest. Let's do it. If we win, we'll use the money for a trip to the capital for the big quilt show."

It requires humility to admit our mistakes to God or others. Our pride structure would rather hide them, but when we own up to them, we help others avoid repeating those errors. A frank look at our failures causes us to ask God's help to not repeat our errors.

⌒⌒

GOD'S PATTERN
God draws close to the humble. When we learn from our mistakes and use them to help others learn, God hears our cries.

BACK TO THE GRINDSTONE

Cindy pursed her lips as she drew her chalk pencil over the green material, marking the design for her Sashiko quilt piece. The white chalk stood out well from the dark background, making her stitching lines easy to follow. Since she had used a simple pattern and her piece was small, she finished before supper. While her roast cooked, she ran over to her Japanese neighbor's house to show Sukey her work. The Sashiko quilts Sukey brought from Japan when she moved from her homeland were Cindy's inspiration for her quilt square.

"Pretty design," Sukey said, "and you made your stitches nice and even. Very good. All that's left is to get rid of these chalk lines." Sukey brushed her hand across the material. Since the chalk remained, she brushed harder.

"Oh, no. The chalk isn't coming off." Cindy tried her hand at brushing. "All that's happening is the chalk spreads wider and wider." When the stubborn chalk remained, she took the material and rubbed it together like she was scrubbing a stain.

"It looks a little better," Sukey encouraged. "You keep on working at it, and the chalk should disappear. It's worked itself down into the fibers. If I'd known you wanted to do Sashiko quilting, I'd have lent you my chalk wheel. Look what a difference it makes." She ran her wheel over another piece of fabric. It made a thin line of chalk dust. "See, the chalk doesn't work into the fabric and will brush right off when you have finished." Sukey brushed the chalk away.

"What a difference the right equipment makes." Cindy picked up the wheel. "May I borrow this to do another piece? Your way is better."

"Sure. The wheel beats grinding the chalk in and scrubbing it out later. Wish I could brush off my daily mistakes with as little trouble. I can't get over the way I yelled at my kids yesterday. Their crime was making too much noise, then I made a whole lot more, yelling at them. I feel like an awful mom." Sukey frowned.

"You need the right spiritual approach," Cindy said. "When a sin makes an ugly mark on us, we can't rub it out by ourselves. But if we go to God and ask forgiveness, He takes away the mark. It's good to ask God for forgiveness right away before the mistake becomes ingrained, creating a pattern of behavior that's hard to erase."

"I'm going to pray right now. Will you pray with me?" Sukey reached for Cindy's hand.

The daily cares of life can grind into our souls and create a smudged outlook. By giving our care to God, we avoid permanent marks.

GOD'S PATTERN

Patterns of repetitive sin sink into our souls,
making sin patterns harder to change.
God's pattern allows us to run
quickly to Him for forgiveness to
prevent sin from becoming entrenched.
Quick repentance keeps sin from
burrowing into our soul and
establishing its pattern over our thinking.

A GIFT

Every man according as he
purposeth in his heart,
so let him give; not grudgingly,
or of necessity:
for God loveth a cheerful giver.
2 CORINTHIANS 9:7 KJV

Carolyn shifted the basket on her arm, took a deep breath, and knocked on the door. She shifted from one foot to the other and rehearsed her request while she waited for her neighbor to answer. She stammered anyway when Mrs. Tatlock opened the door, frowning and wiping flour from her hands onto her apron.

"I'm afraid I've interrupted your baking," Carolyn said, holding a bundle of dried cornflowers and milkweed pods out to the scowling woman. "Would you trade me some material scraps for these dried flowers? I want to give Mother a Christmas present of scraps so she can make a quilt. Don't you think that would make a wonderful gift?" she jabbered, entreating the silent woman towering over her eight-year-old frame. "I hung these flowers in the attic to dry last summer. I think they would make a lovely bouquet for your table."

"Why don't you just make them into a Christmas bouquet for your mother?" Mrs. Tatlock said, her frown lessening.

"Mother can sell a finished quilt, and the money would help with the regress-shins, or is it a depresses-shins? Anyway, she says it doesn't have anything to do with her legs; it's the bad time 1929 brought everyone."

"You mean the Depression." Mrs. Tatlock's face softened. "Yes, 1929 is a hard year. I suppose I do have a few minutes before the bread needs to be punched down for the next rising. You step inside where it's warm, and I'll look in my scrap bag. Sit here." Mrs. Tatlock pulled a chair out from the kitchen table and set a crock in front of Carolyn. "Butter yourself a crust from last week's baking while I look. I declare you look as thin as a scarecrow. Don't you young'uns over there eat enough?" Mrs. Tatlock laid a few pieces of cloth on the table.

"We have lots of potato soup every night." Carolyn slathered a generous portion of butter on her bread. "The cellar's full of potatoes from our garden. Maybe mother will buy some brown sugar and rice with the money from the quilt." Carolyn didn't wait to finish talking before taking a big bite. "Brown sugar would taste good," she mumbled between chews.

Mrs. Tatlock pulled the small drawer out from the corner cabinet, took a clean flour sack from the laundry, and dumped all the scraps from the drawer into it. "Maybe some of these fabrics will look pretty together. What a thoughtful little girl to think of such a good present for your mother."

Thanks to Mrs. Tatlock's generosity, Carolyn only needed to visit a few more of her neighbors before Christmas to accumulate a nice selection of material scraps. While Mother hung clothes outside to dry, she ironed the materials and placed them carefully in Mrs. Tatlock's flour sack. She tied the end together with a red hair ribbon from her drawer.

Her eyes shining with anticipation of her mother's pleasure, Carolyn snuck the gift behind their tree on Christmas Eve. Even the paper chains and popcorn decorations on the tree seemed more lovely as she thought of how much her mother would like her present.

Years later, Carolyn remembered her satisfaction hearing

her mother's exclamations of delight over the gift of scraps. After each child opened a handmade gift from their mother or father, the whole family enjoyed spreading out the fabric pieces and sorting them by color. Carolyn's eyes still fill with tears when she remembers Mother selling the quilt she made using the Wild Goose pattern for enough money to buy Carolyn her first brand-new shoes. Shoes her older sisters had not worn first. Shoes decorated with shiny patent leather bows.

Looking back as an adult, Carolyn wondered if her mother was really as delighted to receive a bag of rags for a Christmas gift as her childish eyes thought, or if Mother was a supreme actor. Regardless, Carolyn's mother turned the rags into a form of riches for her daughter.

GOD'S PATTERN

God loves for us to give with enthusiasm.
He always gives us more joy than
we expected when we throw our hearts
into giving to others.

QUILTING
TIPS

Before washing fabric, use the serger sewing machine
to stitch the edges of your material to prevent fraying.

To store an old quilt, use a prewashed white pillowcase.

Because of the chemical process of manufacturing silk, it rots faster
than other material. Avoid silk if you want a lasting quilt.

For small quilts, hold the three layers of the top, batting, and
backing together with lots of safety pins instead of basting thread
to keep them from "wandering" apart.

Attach your quilt label on the back before you quilt the layers
together. The quilt stitches will integrate the label into the project
and prevent anyone from removing it later.

At quilt shows, the staff handles quilts with white gloves to
prevent soiling the items. Wearing clean white gloves
is a good way to handle any precious heirloom quilts.

*When painting or writing on fabric, check to make sure
that the paints are permanent and won't wash out.
Ironing helps set fabric paint.*

⌘

*Old scraps work well for patterns that suggest
antiquity because they have been used for centuries.*

⌘

*When many people are contributing to one quilt,
make one person responsible for cutting all the foundation
squares to ensure they are exactly the same size.*

⌘

*When storing quilts, refold them periodically. The folds
falling in a different place prevents them from
causing a permanent mark on the quilt.*

⌘

*When the quilting process seems long, think about
something pleasant to make the time pass faster. Try
contemplating the character of God.*

⌘

*Machine quilting is a good way to overcome time pressures.
The machine gives a more distinct indentation. If the
material ripples, adjust the pressure.*

Pushing the fabric from underneath helps the
needle take a smaller bite and keeps the stitches smaller.

∞

For perfect matching when machine sewing,
use very fine pins and sew over them.

∞

Many photocopy shops do an excellent
job of transferring photographs to fabric.

∞

The pattern on the "wrong side," or the back side,
of the fabric often carries a more subtle color or pattern
that may enhance a quilt better than the right side.

∞

Arrange choices of fabric together and then stand at a
distance from them to judge how well they blend together.

∞

To create a warm blanket, substitute a length of wool
for the usual polyfill as the middle layer of a quilt.

*To hide a knot, tug it through the top
of the quilt and into the batting.*

*White fabric or paper behind the eye of a needle
makes it easier to see when threading it.*

*To protect fingers from soreness, use a
layer of masking or adhesive tape.*

*A&D Ointment, Vick's salve, or an antibiotic
ointment all help sore hands heal overnight.*

Be open to trying new techniques and equipment.

*Relax your hands, arms, and shoulders when doing free motion
quilting on a machine. This allows a creative flow of fabric under
the needle and encourages evenly spaced stitches.*

Sharp scissors help cutting accuracy.

*A magnet attached to a long handle helps
pick up pins from the floor.*

*If you are caught without a thimble, use the
inside of your forefinger nail to push the needle through
and the top of a fingernail underneath the quilt to
glance the needle off toward the top again.*

*When sewing many squares together on the machine, instead of
cutting the thread at the end of each piece, begin sewing the next
two squares together. Chain stitch in this manner until all the
squares are finished. Cutting them apart later saves time.*

Use a rotary cutter for a better finished product when piecing.

*A small photo of the quilt maker photocopied onto fabric and sewn
to the back as part of a quilt label makes a nice memory jogger.*

Old blankets can be used for the middle of a quilt.

*Check the full width of a piece of material to determine
that there are no flaws, and choose tightly woven fabric
for a quilt that will wear well.*

*To mark using a template, begin marking at one corner and
proceed to the middle and then begin at the opposite corner
and mark to the middle again to prevent stretching.*

*To control pests, periodically check quilts that are
stored in dark, warm places. Occasionally shake them
out and air them while vacuuming the area.*

Quilting with someone makes the time go faster.

Always use cold water for bloodstains. An ice cube works.

By signing one's name in pencil and then embroidering over it, not only is the name recorded but a sample of the person's handwriting is preserved.

To remove the lines made with a water-soluble pencil, spray with a mist bottle filled with cold water.

When vacuuming a quilt to remove dust, make a Fiberglass screen and cover the rough edges with tape. By placing the screen over the quilt you will not suck the fabric into the vacuum.

Many judges disqualify a quilt for a show if they find cat or dog hair on it!

A good way to store inherited quilts is to roll them on a long fabric-covered tube.

A color wheel, often available in paint stores, helps determine which colors provide the most light and dark contrast.

A vinegar rinse helps set colors applied to fabric.
Place waxed paper over a crayon drawing
on a fabric and iron to set the color.

❧

Check with the library, YWCA, or quilting
supply stores to find local quilting guilds.

❧

To establish order, draw a grain direction line on each template
and organize the templates by storing the ones for each project in a
plastic bag together with a drawing of the pattern.

❧

To document a quilt made by a group, use a pie-shaped label. Each
wedge may be signed by a person and appliquéd with a flower
using a dominant fabric from the person's block.

❧

For a quilt square swap, each person in the group makes
the same square enough times for every person to receive one.
The squares are distributed, and everyone uses them to
create her own quilt with a nice variety of squares
and a lasting souvenir of each person.

❧

Narrow bias binding works best on curves.

*Running a thread through beeswax helps
prevent knots, raveling, and tangles.*

❧

*Lay tiny pieces of material on paper to see in advance
how a block will look. Rearrange the pieces until
satisfied and then glue them in place as a reference.*

❧

*When appliquéing for a quilt top, stitch fusible bonding to the right
side of the piece one-fourth inch inside the pattern edge, then slit the
bonding, turn right sides out, and iron in place. This holds the piece
without pins for the appliquéing.*

❧

*To research a quilt's history, check your local library. Many libraries
contain books organized by states, periods, and design.*

❧

*A touch of stick lip balm makes thread
easier to punch through the eye of a needle.*

❧

*There's hope if you find grease marks on fabric.
Shampoo for oily hair will often remove the stain.*

To comfort sore fingers, quilters may soak them in a mixture of magnesium salts and warm water or in alum water.

Burlap is an inferior fabric for backing. Do not choose too loose a material for backing nor one so dense it is hard to sew through. Take a needle to the store when selecting fabric and see how easy it is to run the needle through the material.

To keep finished squares flat and safe from damage, use new, clean pizza boxes to store them until you are ready to put them together.

Use a spot remover like Lestoil at full strength on spots such as blood, tomato, makeup, or chocolate. Put a clean white towel underneath to prevent the stain from spreading.

If a material has been scorched by ironing, dip it in weak tea to conceal the spot.

Make a sandpaper board by gluing a sheet of sandpaper on Plexiglas. The board holds fabric still for cutting.

To air a quilt, place it on a mattress pad or several sheets and cover it with another sheet to prevent fading and protect it from debris. Place it outdoors in the shade.

When marking for echo quilting, use dots instead of a line. Dots don't pull the fabric or cause distortion.

Avoid washing or dry cleaning a treasured quilt whenever possible.

Select good quality material for a quilt backing to help the quilt wear well.

When large numbers of people contribute to the same quilt, one way to record their participation is to sign a cotton twill tape with their names, which can then be sewn to one edge of the quilt backing.

A long doll-making needle is a good instrument to pull cording through a trapunto design.

To prevent sore fingers, limit the time of each quilting session and alternate with other activities for a rest.

As you finish one portion of a quilt, remove the "ugly" basting threads as a small reward and a motivation to continue the next portion with its ugly basting thread.

If we think about the problems women of previous generations encountered while we stitch, our difficulties will fall into a healthy perspective.

Don't try to stack more than four pieces for cutting together, and secure them with a pin to prevent shifting.

Thread a whole pack of needles at once onto one spool of thread. Knot the end to prevent them from falling off. Each time you need new thread, pull the required length through a needle before cutting the thread from the spool and knotting the end again.

Garage sales, flea markets, estate sales, and store discount tables make good places to stock up on bargain fabric for backings.

Maintain balance when using extra bright colors by spreading them here and there throughout the entire quilt.

Do not attempt to learn quilting with a difficult pattern. Begin with a simple design that will ensure success.

For an attractive quilt, select a print for the backing that reinforces the theme of the front.

In order to stay motivated to finish a project, allow yourself regular breaks to stand and stretch.

Stop while quilting to exercise hands by alternating finger stretches with making fists. Quilt shops carry stretchy, fingerless gloves to keep arthritic hands warm.

Measure the quilt for a binding by using either dental floss or macrame string because they won't stretch.

Allow the quilting pattern to reflect the design of the pieced blocks such as stitches following a flower design or a feather pattern for a quilt including birds.

When a hole requires mending, cut a piece of fabric into a design that coordinates with the theme of the quilt. The patch will appear to be part of the plan.

Since fabrics are discontinued regularly, always buy extra in case you need more than anticipated later.

Mark the front cover of your quilting magazines with the page number of any ideas you'd like to try someday.

A bodkin helps move small pieces under the presser foot when machine stitching.

When ironed, freezer paper will stick to fabric.

Our saliva contains an enzyme that neutralizes the proteins of our own blood. To remove a bloodstain, moisten a cotton swab in your mouth and rub the blemish.

When hanging an old quilt, be sure to support its weight. Quilt clips are available through quilt stores.

A silver pencil works well for marking quilting lines on dark material.

White tailor's chalk on dark fabric comes off easily.

To preserve a quilt that requires folding for storage, use generous amounts of acid-free tissue paper in each fold to prevent creases.

Quilters generously share their knowledge. Don't hesitate to ask for help from quilting stores and accomplished quilters.